REHARMONIZATION
TECHNIQUES

RANDY FELTS

Berklee Media

Associate Vice President: Dave Kusek
Director of Content: Debbie Cavalier
Marketing Manager: Jennifer Rassler
Senior Graphic Designer: David Ehlers

Berklee Press

Senior Writer/Editor: Jonathan Feist
Writer/Editor: Susan Gedutis
Production Manager: Shawn Girsberger

ISBN 0-634-01585-0

1140 Boylston Street
Boston, MA 02215-3693 USA
(617) 747-2146

Visit Berklee Press Online at
www.berkleepress.com

DISTRIBUTED BY

HAL•LEONARD®
CORPORATION
7777 W. BLUEMOUND RD. P.O. BOX 13819
MILWAUKEE, WISCONSIN 53213

Visit Hal Leonard Online at
www.halleonard.com

ACKNOWLEDGMENTS AND DEDICATION

I dedicate this book to my wife Nancy and daughter Susannah. Their love is a source of continuous inspiration and joy.

I would also like to express sincere gratitude to my mother Dorothy Harris Felts, brother Robert Franklin Felts, and all the other members of my extended clan for their support and encouragement through many years.

This book is based upon the concepts developed in the Berklee College of Music Harmony Department. I am forever in the debt of the many contributors, both past and present, to this system of popular music analysis. I hope to continue lively dialogs with this wonderful group of teachers and scholars for many years to come.

Many thanks to Dave Olsen, Director of Business Affairs at Warner Bros. Publications, for his assistance in securing copyrights for songs used in this book. I also would like to extend a special word of thanks to my editors at Berklee Press, Susan Gedutis and Debbie Cavalier, for their untiring work, sharp eyes, and good humor.

INTRODUCTION

Reharmonization is the musical equivalent of a new paint job on an old car. When you reharmonize a tune, you provide new color to it by altering the harmonic progression that supports its melody.

Whether you write jingles, film scores, or soundtracks for video games, you will find ideas in this book that you can use. If you are a band or choir director you will find simple, effective ideas to update the songs in your next show. If you play solo piano or guitar, you can use these concepts to develop new arrangements of the songs in your set list. Composers and arrangers can use these ideas to easily create harmonic variations of their themes.

I have refined the techniques and concepts presented in this book during my twenty-four years as an instructor of jazz harmony at Berklee College of Music in Boston, Mass. Though this book was written for use in the reharmonization techniques course at Berklee, it is designed to help players of any musical background understand the reharmonization process. Instrumental virtuosity is not required!

Throughout my musical career, I have built upon concepts from jazz and pop music theory to create what I call a "musical toolbox." Each theory concept represents a tool. Once you understand how the tools work, you can use them to create new chord changes. These new chord changes act as harmonic "beds" that support melodic material. They can alter the mood of the original melody in creative and interesting ways, and may be used in many musical styles.

What You Need to Know

To get the most from the book, you must be familiar with common chord symbols and their inversions, and you should be able to play music notated in lead sheet format on guitar or keyboard. You will also need to know how to read music in both treble and bass clefs and be familiar with key signatures of all the major and minor keys.

How to Use This Book

The first twelve chapters present reharmonization techniques that work well with traditional, mainstream pop and jazz. The last four chapters point to more recent film music and contemporary jazz styles. Many of the chapters are narrow in focus and cover a specific concept that is easy to understand. Other chapters are broader in focus and discuss techniques that may require substantial practice to master.

If you have never reharmonized melodies or used music theory to explore the potential of musical phrases, I suggest that you first read and do the exercises for the first five chapters. Then, practice these new ideas with music in your repertoire until you feel comfortable applying these concepts. Once you have some experience, check out the later chapters, which combine multiple concepts.

If you have a lot of reharmonization/harmonic experience, you may want to jump directly to chapters 13–16 and then backtrack to the ideas found in the earlier chapters.

Each chapter contains exercises that will help you apply each reharmonization concept. As you complete the exercises in each chapter, be sure to check out the reference examples in the back of this book to see if you're on the right track.

ONWARD!

This book presents a series of starting points for exploration. The reharmonization techniques presented work most successfully after a period of experimentation, reflection, and feedback from other musicians.

ABOUT THE AUTHOR

 Randy Felts is an Associate Professor in the Harmony Department at Berklee College of Music in Boston. He has taught at the college since 1976. He performs regularly on saxophone, flute, and Synthophone in contexts ranging from classic 1960s rock to original jazz and pop music. Randy is the U.S. representative for Softwind Instruments, manufacturers of the Synthophone, an alto saxophone that allows the performer to play sounds contained in any MIDI-capable keyboard or sound module using normal saxophone fingerings, breath, and lip control.

CONTENTS

SIMPLE SUBSTITUTION

If reharmonizing a tune is like painting a car, then simple substitution is like choosing a different shade of the same color—going from blue to indigo, or rose to pink. Simple substitution involves replacing a chord with another that has similar harmonic function. It allows you to change the sound of a tune while still retaining much of its original color.

In order to use simple substitution as a reharmonization technique, you must understand the division of the seven diatonic chords into three groups or **families**. Each of these chord families has a **function**. A chord's function is its tendency to move or remain stable within a musical phrase. Let's use the key of C as an example.

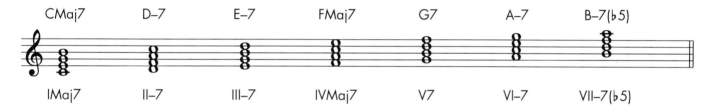

Fig. 1.1. Diatonic seventh chords in the key of C

TONIC FAMILY   ANALYSIS SYMBOL: (T)

The **tonic** family of chords has a resting function. Chords in this group tend to sound stable. They have little sense of forward motion and are almost always found at the phrase endings of popular and standard tunes. Diatonic chords built on the first, third, and sixth degrees of a scale are the members of this group.

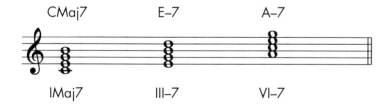

Fig. 1.2. Tonic family (T) chords in the key of C

Tonic chords share several common tones. The chords are considered restful because they do not contain the fourth degree of the scale, which is F in the key of C. The fourth degree of any major scale is known as a **tendency tone**—it tends to lead to the third degree of the scale when played over IMaj7.

SUBDOMINANT FAMILY   ANALYSIS SYMBOL: (SD)

Chords in the **subdominant** family have a moderate tendency to move ahead within the musical phrase. All chords in this family contain the restless fourth degree of the scale. Chords built on the second and fourth scale degrees make up this group. The V7sus4 is also included in this family, because it contains the fourth scale degree instead of the third. (Using a suspended fourth instead of a third eliminates the tritone that gives a dominant family chord its characteristic sound. The tritone function is described below.)

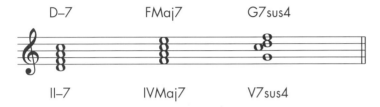

Fig. 1.3. Subdominant family (SD) chords in the key of C

DOMINANT FAMILY   ANALYSIS SYMBOL: (D)

Chords in the **dominant** family sound unresolved and have a strong tendency toward resolution. They are said to have a "moving" function. Dominant chords almost always precede phrase endings in popular and standard tunes. The chords V7, VII–7(♭5), and V7sus4 are in this family. (The V7sus4 chord has a dominant function when it resolves directly to IMaj7, even though it lacks the tritone interval.)

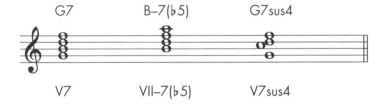

Fig. 1.4. Dominant family (D) chords in the key of C

V7 and VII–7(♭5) share many common tones. They also contain both the fourth and seventh scale degrees. The intervallic distance between these two notes is called a **tritone**, also known as an **augmented** fourth. The tritone's highly restless sound produces a strong sense of forward motion. The tritone formed by the third and seventh of a dominant chord creates the chord's strong forward motion. Dominant family chords often resolve to a chord in the tonic family.

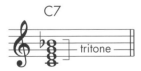

Fig. 1.5. C7 chord with its tritone interval

How Simple Substitution Works

The following examples explore how simple substitution works.

Fig. 1.6. A basic model

Below, simple substitution modifies the model. Note that the chord function is kept the same in each measure. Look closely at the musical example to:

1. Verify the functional analysis of each chord in the original phrase.

2. Observe the substitution of other chords that have a similar function in the key.

Fig. 1.7. Simple substitution modifies the basic model

Fig. 1.8. Simple substitution, another variation

The following examples apply simple substitution to a phrase from the jazz standard, "Here's That Rainy Day." Notice the functional analysis of each chord in the original phrase.

Fig. 1.9. "Here's That Rainy Day" (J. Van Heusen/J. Burke), original form

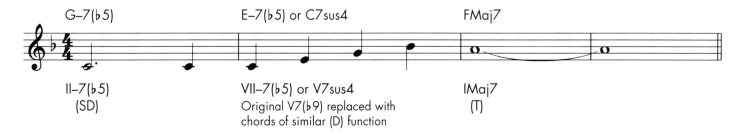

Fig. 1.10. "Here's That Rainy Day," dominant chord replaced by another chord in its family

Fig. 1.11. "Here's That Rainy Day," tonic chord replaced by another chord in its family

MELODY/HARMONY RELATIONSHIPS

When using these substitutions, pay close attention to the **melody/harmony relationship**—the intervals created between the notes in the melody and the notes in the supporting chord. Sometimes, the notes in the new substitute chord can clash with the melody.

UNWANTED ♭9 INTERVALS

Avoid unwanted ♭9 (or ♭2) melody/harmony intervals when using simple substitution. The ♭2 interval is a half step. It is also known as a ♭9, which is an octave plus a minor second. This melody/harmony interval creates a dissonance strong enough to destroy the basic function of the chord. In general, avoid choosing a substitute chord that creates a ♭9 interval with any one of the melody notes.

The V7(♭9) is the only common exception to this rule. The V7(♭9) has become an acceptable sound in many pop and jazz songs. For example, a C7♭9 moving to FMaj7 in the key of F major works because the ♭9 is combined with a tritone interval. Both the ♭9 and tritone intervals follow established melodic tendencies when they resolve to the Fmaj7. Many listeners perceive ♭9 combinations that do not follow such well-established paths of resolution as errors or wrong notes.

In the following example, the III–7 creates an unwanted ♭9 interval in the melody, also referred to as **"in the lead."** The last melody note, F, forms a ♭9 with E, which is the fifth of the A–7 chord. The chord has a minor quality and as such cannot be clearly understood if used with a ♭9 melody/harmony combination.

Fig. 1.12. Unwanted ♭9 melody/harmony relationship

UNWANTED TRITONE INTERVALS

Avoid unwanted tritone (♯4/♯11) melody/harmony intervals on minor seventh chords.

Fig. 1.13. Original form

Below, in measure 2, the B in the lead of D–7 creates an unwanted tritone interval with F, the third of the chord. This tritone melody/harmony combination destroys the chord's original function, transforming D–7 from a subdominant chord into an odd-sounding dominant structure. The resulting sound is dissonant and awkward in a simple diatonic context; the interval combination doesn't blend or resolve smoothly within the phrase.

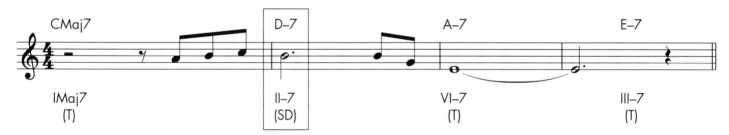

Fig. 1.14. Unwanted tritone melody/harmony relationship

It is interesting that the IVMaj7 chord (FMaj7) can be used with ♯4 in the melody, while its simple substitution, II–7(D–7), does not work as effectively with the same melody/harmony combination—even though both chords share subdominant function.

Most pop writers adhere to the unspoken rule of not using ♯4 intervals on minor seventh chords because it can create too great a change in the sound and character of the original chord. To the listener—even to the nonmusician—the FMaj7 with B in the lead sounds subtly less awkward than D–7 with B in the lead.

The use of 13 in the lead of minor seventh chords, which produces a tritone with the third, is even more awkward when the minor seventh is a II–7 followed by V7. The musical flow of the cadence seems more satisfying when the tritone interval and its greater sense of motion are reserved for the G7. Avoid using a 13 or ♭13 in the lead of II–7 chords.

Another general rule to follow when reharmonizing popular tunes: keep it simple.

Once you have chosen your primary chord substitutions, you can add additional chords to help smooth out the progression. Adding chords increases the number of chords used in each bar. This is referred to as increasing the **harmonic rhythm**.

In general, more active harmonic rhythms produce a more energetic musical phrase, while slower harmonic rhythms are more languid. Evaluate the effect of different harmonic rhythms with every musical example you encounter.

The example below reharmonizes the melody of fig. 1.6 using simple substitution and doubling the number of chords per measure. This gives the progression a "busier" feel. The chord inversion (A–7/E) smoothes the transition between the two tonic chords.

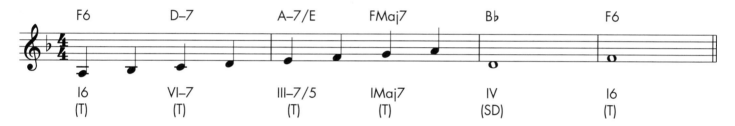

Fig. 1.15. Simple substitution and faster harmonic rhythm

Jazz standards and bebop tunes, which commonly use two or more chords per measure, have fast harmonic rhythm. In contrast, in contemporary pop styles, a single chord may last for many measures.

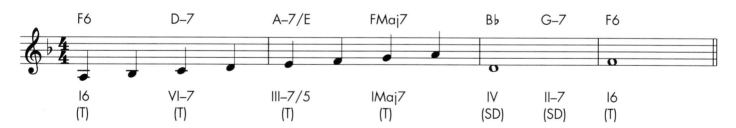

Fig. 1.16. Jazz- or bebop-style harmonic rhythm

Exercises

Reharmonize the examples using simple substitution. Use both slow and fast harmonic rhythm in developing your reharmonizations. Label each chord with a Roman numeral (IMaj7, II–7, etc.), and label each chord with its functional family name: tonic (T), subdominant (SD), or dominant (D). The first example is done for you. After trying some chord substitutions of your own, check out the reference examples at the end of the book.

Note: It is not necessary to change all of the original chords to get an interesting reharmonization.

EXERCISE 1.1

Original form with Roman numeral analysis:

Your reharmonization 1:

Your reharmonization 2:

EXERCISE 1.2

Original form with Roman numeral analysis:

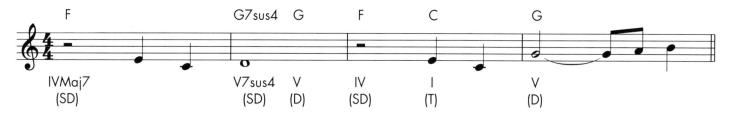

Your reharmonization 1:

Your reharmonization 2:

Continue reharmonizing these examples using simple substitution. Use the same analysis procedures as on the previous page.

EXERCISE 1.3

Original form with Roman numeral analysis:

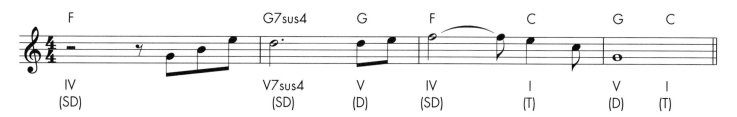

Your reharmonization 1:

Your reharmonization 2:

EXERCISE 1.4

Original form with Roman numeral analysis:

Your reharmonization 1:

Your reharmonization 2:

2

DIATONIC APPROACH

Chords may be approached by other chords that share the same key—known as **diatonic** chords. This reharmonization method, referred to as **diatonic approach** technique, keeps the tune largely within a single key. Diatonic approach technique works well when you wish to introduce a more active harmonic rhythm and some harmonic variety to a tune without losing the tonal color of the original phrase. It works well with song phrases that are also diatonic, such as those found in mainstream country, pop, and folk styles.

Diatonic approach technique is derived from the practice of jazz and pop arrangers, who often reharmonize a series of melodic quarter notes that lead into a target chord. (This technique can sometimes be used to support other melodic shapes. Examples will appear later in this chapter.)

Diatonic chords are created by layering thirds above each pitch in a scale.

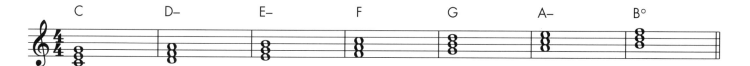

Fig. 2.1. Diatonic triads in C major

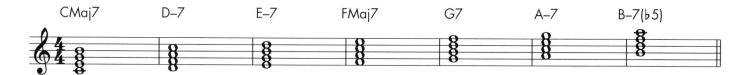

Fig. 2.2. Diatonic seventh chords in C major

To have an approach, one must have a destination. A harmonic destination is referred to as a **target chord**. It is a critical structural element in the musical phrase. While any chord in a progression may be thought of as a potential target chord, successful target chords are often the last or next-to-last chords of a phrase.

The short example below illustrates a diatonic melody that is a good candidate for diatonic approach technique. The last chord is the target since it represents the end of the phrase in the key of C major. It is common to use the last chord of a phrase as a target chord.

Fig. 2.3. Identify the target chord.

CADENCES

Movements from chord to chord at important phrase locations are called **cadences**. Cadences carry musical momentum. It is useful to think of them as "nodes" of musical energy that lead to resting points in the musical phrase.

On a simple level, song phrases are like jokes told by a stand-up comedian. As the comedian moves from joke to joke, the cadence is like the setup point just before each punch line. Just as great comedians practice their timing, the exact location of a musical cadence requires coordination with the melodic line and a developed sense of harmonic rhythm. Fortunately, the average listener has an intuitive feel for the placement of cadences from long exposure to the conventions of pop music. (To explore these ideas in more detail, check *Melody in Songwriting: Tools and Techniques for Writing Hit Songs* by Jack Perricone, Berklee Press.)

The traditional definition of cadence emphasizes the resolution of tendency tones 4 to 3 and 7 to 1. My definition is somewhat nontraditional, but it serves our purposes in the context of developing reharmonization choices.

Cadences come in several flavors: **strong**, **weak**, and **deceptive**. Strong and weak cadences play a significant role in diatonic approach technique and will be discussed in the examples to follow. While deceptive cadences play no role in diatonic approach technique, they are listed here because they are important to techniques presented in subsequent chapters.

STRONG CADENCES

Strong cadences produce a dramatic sense of resolution into a target chord. They produce sharp contrast and are often used to approach target chords at phrase endings. Strong cadences are created whenever the **approach chord** (the chord immediately preceding the target) and the target chord share no more than two pitches. The general rule is: strong cadences = few common tones between the cadential chord and its target.

The number of common tones between chords is associated with the root motion between them. **Diatonic** chords whose roots are a third or a sixth apart have many common tones. Diatonic chords whose roots are not a third or a sixth apart have fewer common tones.

For example, there are two notes in FMaj7 that are not found in CMaj7: F and A. These two notes result in a distinct contrast between the two chords. Accordingly, the cadence from FMaj7 to CMaj7 is strong.

Most often, a strong cadence is used to approach a target chord. The choice of which diatonic approach chord to use is influenced by the relationship of the melody note to the chord and by the root motion of the approach chord into the target.

In order to retain a diatonic sound, the melodic lead of the approach chord must be a chord tone—1, 3, 5, or 7.

Figure 2.4 shows FMaj7 with an A in the lead moving into the target chord. The melody/harmony relationship is a third, and the chord and melody notes are diatonic. In addition, the root motion between FMaj7 and CMaj7 is a perfect fourth, ensuring that at least two different pitches will be sounded during the cadence. Therefore, Fmaj7 is a good choice as a diatonic approach chord to CMaj7.

Fig. 2.4. Strong cadence

WEAK CADENCES

Weak cadences, also referred to as gentle cadences, are produced when the approach chord and the target chord have three or more notes in common. Because the chord tones are so similar, weak cadences produce a subtle change in the flow of the progression. Weak cadences are sometimes found in phrase endings, but may be found more often at the beginning or midsections of a phrase. Weak cadences happen whenever the roots of the approach chord and the target chord are a **diatonic** third or a **diatonic** sixth apart.

Fig. 2.5. Weak cadence

DECEPTIVE CADENCES

Deceptive cadences are produced when a dominant seventh chord moves unexpectedly. For example, a V7 chord is expected to resolve by perfect fifth to I major. Motion from the V7 to any chord other than IMaj7 is "deceptive."

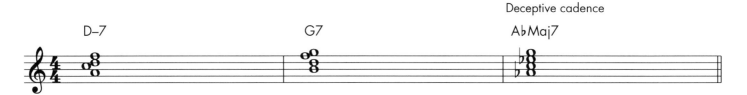

Fig. 2.6. Deceptive cadence

(See chapter 9 for more on deceptive cadences.)

MELODY/HARMONY RELATIONSHIPS

To reharmonize using diatonic approach technique, first choose a target chord and an approach chord. Once you have chosen an approach chord, notice the melody/harmony relationship. Below, the A in the lead of the A–7 produces a unison melody/harmony relationship. That is, the root of the chord is in the lead melodic position. Working backwards from the cadential approach chord, I support each of the remaining melody notes with a chord, making sure each of the chords is **diatonic** to the key and that each chord has a **root** in the lead.

Fig. 2.7. Working backwards from the target chord, all chords are diatonic and have 1 in the lead.

This example exposes a potential weakness of this technique: an extremely active harmonic rhythm. Active harmonic rhythm can easily sound overdone or too busy. You can avoid a hyperactive harmonic rhythm by limiting yourself to short "runs" of notes approaching a target chord. See the shorter, less active variation below.

Fig. 2.8. Less active harmonic rhythm

Accompany each melody note with a diatonic chord that maintains the same melody/harmony relationship. In the next example, I maintain a melody/harmony relationship of a third, keeping 3 in the lead of each chord.

Fig. 2.9. Working backwards from the target chord, all chords are diatonic and have 3 in the lead.

There is one nondiatonic chord that may be used with diatonic approach technique, the ♭VIIMaj7. In the key of C, the ♭VIIMaj7 is B♭Maj7. It produces a rich sound without over-powering other diatonic chords.

Though the B♭Maj7 chord is not diatonic to C major, it blends smoothly with the other diatonic choices. That is because the B♭Maj7 is diatonic to the C Dorian scale, a key that is **parallel** to C major. The key is called parallel because C major and C Dorian begin on the same pitch, but contain different whole- and half-step combinations. C Dorian is a modal scale and has a minor quality.

Since B♭Maj7 is derived from this parallel minor scale, it is described as darker than B–7(♭5), which is derived from the brighter-sounding C major scale. This slightly darker choice works well as a substitute for B–7♭5 in instances where all other chord choices are diatonic.

Diatonic texture is derived from a single scale or key. By limiting the lead of a diatonic approach chord to 1, 3, 5, or 7, one can be sure that the texture of the phrase will remain diatonic. The sound is homogenous and smooth. Play and listen to the following examples.

Fig. 2.10. Working backwards from the target chord, all chords except for the ♭VIIMaj7 are diatonic and all three of them have 3 in the lead.

Fig. 2.11. Approach chords have a melody/harmony relationship of a fifth, and 5 in the lead of each diatonic chord.

Fig. 2.12. Approach chords maintain a melody/harmony relationship of a seventh, and scale degree 7 is in the lead.

On rare occasions, you may be able to use melody/harmony relationships of a ninth, eleventh, or thirteenth (with 9, 11, or 13 in the lead, respectively) without destroying the diatonic color of the original phrase. The next examples illustrate these possibilities.

In fig. 2.13, the G7 forms a strong cadence to the CMaj7 target chord.

Fig. 2.13. Almost all chords are diatonic and have 9 in the lead.

In the next example, I employ the diatonic approach technique using an 11 in the lead of each chord. Notice that this melody/harmony combination could only be produced by working backwards from E–7. The E–7 chord produces a weak cadence into the CMaj7 target chord.

Fig. 2.14. Almost all chords are diatonic and have 11 in the lead.

The use of 9, 11, or 13 in the lead greatly increases the possibility that the progression will quickly move out of the original key. It also means that you will more frequently encounter unwanted melody/harmony relationships, such as dissonant ♭9 or ♯11 intervals. Though the result may sound interesting, its chromatic sound may be too dissonant for use in a mainstream pop style. To maintain a truly diatonic texture, restrict your choice of melody/harmony combinations to 1, 3, 5, or 7 in the lead of the diatonic chords.

Using chords outside the original key introduces more extreme forms of color into the harmonic "bed." Evaluate each phrase carefully to determine whether your harmonic choices work well with the melody and blend smoothly in a stylistic sense with the other phrases in the reharmonized song. (Techniques that use nondiatonic chords are discussed at length in following chapters.) No matter which technique you use, always avoid poor melody/harmony combinations—unwanted ♭9s and tritones.

In the example below, a diatonic chord approaches the target chord (CMaj7), using the melody note A as a 13. This choice produces another CMaj7. Since the approach chord is identical to the target chord, there is no contrast and therefore no cadence. This poor choice produces an ineffective ending and sets in motion a series of clashes between the chords and the melody.

In this example, using consistent 13s in the lead produces a series of unwanted melody/harmony combinations. C in the lead of E–7 produces an unwanted ♭9 interval, and B on D–7 produces an unwanted tritone with the F in the D–7 chord. Melody/harmony errors are indicated with an "x".

Fig. 2.15. Almost all chords are diatonic and have 13 in the lead, producing unwanted melody/harmony relationships.

Although diatonic approach technique is most often used with quarter-note melodic rhythms, it is also possible to apply it to melodies that have other rhythmic shapes.

Fig. 2.16. Original form

To reharmonize, diatonic chords (and a ♭VIIMaj7) with 3 in the lead support melody notes that fall on rhythmic downbeats. I do not harmonize melodic notes that fall on weaker rhythmic beats. This approach maintains the mostly diatonic texture without having to use busy eighth-note harmonic rhythms.

Fig. 2.17. Working backwards from the target, almost all chords are diatonic and have 3 in the lead.

In fig. 2.18 below, E♭Maj7 (the ♭VIIMaj7 substitute for VII–7(♭5)) is the approach chord to the FMaj7 target chord. The D in the lead of E♭Maj7 is a 7. Working backwards, a diatonic chord supports each melody note that falls on a downbeat. The melody/harmony relationship in each case is a seventh.

Fig. 2.18. *Working backwards from the target, almost all chords are diatonic and have 7 in the lead.*

The next example, with major 7 in the lead, has fewer chords but still maintains a melody/harmony relationship of a seventh in primary rhythmic positions. The less active harmonic rhythm gives the phrase a more relaxed sound.

Fig. 2.19. *Working backwards from the target, almost all chords are diatonic and have 7 in the lead.*

Use the example below as a guide for your own reharmonizations.

Fig. 2.20. *"I Could Write a Book" (R. Rodgers/L. Hart), original form*

Here is a reharmonization using diatonic approach technique.

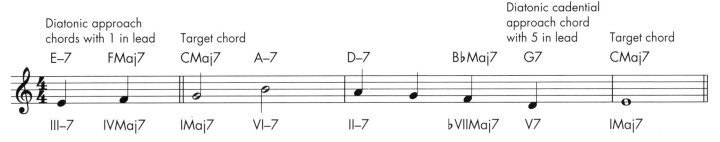

Fig. 2.21. *"I Could Write a Book" reharmonized*

EXERCISES

Use diatonic approach technique to reharmonize the following melodic phrases. Show a Roman numeral analysis of your reharmonizations in all examples that follow. Use 1, 3, 5, and 7 in the lead. After trying some chord substitutions of your own, check out the reference examples at the end of this book. Refer to fig. 2.20 as the original form for this exercise.

EXERCISE 2.1

Your reharmonization 1:

Your reharmonization 2:

Your reharmonization 3:

Reharmonize the following melodic phrases. Consider using patterns that have 9, 11, or 13 in the lead. Remember that melodic patterns using 9, 11, or 13 make it more difficult to maintain a diatonic phrase.

EXERCISE 2.2
"Lydia's Fortune" (R. Felts), original form

Your reharmonization 1:

Your reharmonization 2:

Your reharmonization 3:

Your reharmonization 4:

TRITONE SUBSTITUTION, EXTENDED DOMINANT SEVENTH CHORDS, AND EXTENDED II-V7 PATTERNS

An **extended dominant seventh chord progression** is a series of dominant seventh chords that move forward using downward root motion of a perfect fifth or a minor second. For example, C7–F7–B♭7–E♭7, or C7–B7–B♭7–A7–A♭7.

Extended dominants may be applied to many of the same melodic situations as diatonic approach technique. A phrase harmonized with extended dominant sevenths will quickly move out of its original key and create a "patterned" sound that is highly organized. Playing and listening to a few examples of extended dominant chords will quickly etch this sound into your ear.

TRITONE SUBSTITUTION

Every dominant seventh chord may be substituted, or is interchangeable, with the dominant seventh whose root is a tritone higher. As a reminder, a tritone is an interval of three whole steps. You may also calculate the distance between the roots of these chords as a ♯4 or ♭5 interval, instead of thinking of whole steps or tritones.

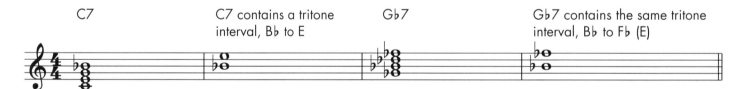

Fig. 3.1. Tritone substitution of C7 is G♭7

To use tritone substitution, start with a target chord. Then, work backward from the target chord, harmonizing each melody note with a series of dominant seventh chords a perfect fifth apart. The next example shows this preliminary step.

Fig. 3.2. Tritone substitution, step 1: dominant seventh chords a fifth apart

Next, analyze and listen to the following example. You will notice a number of melody/harmony clashes. The melody/harmony clashes are marked with an "x" and numbered.

Fig. 3.3. Tritone substitution, step 2: identify melody/harmony clashes

Fig. 3.3 Error	Description
Error 1	The use of B♭ in the melody here functions as a major 7 melody note over a dominant seventh chord. This creates an unwanted dissonant ♭9 (minor 2) interval with the ♭7 chord tone (A).
Error 2	♭13 in the melody moving up. (Flatted/lowered tensions tend to move down.*)
Error 3	Melody note D functions as an 11 on a dominant seventh chord, creating an unwanted ♭9 melody/harmony relationship with the A7 chord's third degree, C♯.
Error 4	♭9 in the melody moving up. (Flatted/lowered tensions tend to move down.*)
Error 5	♯9 in the melody moving up. (Flatted/lowered tensions tend to move down.*)

*Chord tensions are called **altered** when they are a half step above or below a 5, major 9, or a major 13. In the performance practice of pop and jazz standard tunes, altered tensions such as the ♭9, ♯9, ♭5, ♭13 melody notes have *most* often been resolved in a downward direction. Errors 2, 4, and 5 are all examples of altered tensions that violate this **tendency**.

Almost any motion up or down from ♭9, ♯9, ♭5, or ♭13 is possible. However, if you go against the downward tendency of these pitches, you should do so only after carefully listening to the whole phrase to evaluate the blend of melody and chord tones in context. In most music, moving these notes up is an exception, not the norm.

The next example uses tritone substitutions to clear up the melody/harmony errors. In two instances, a sus4 chord was used instead of a regular dominant chord to prevent the additional clash of 11 against the 3.

Fig. 3.4. Tritone substitution: no errors

EXTENDED DOMINANTS

The strong sense of forward motion and resolution created by reharmonizing with chains of extended dominants helps drive short runs of notes toward a target chord. As with diatonic approach technique, be careful not to overuse this method, since it can produce a very busy harmonic rhythm that overpowers the melody.

Fig. 3.5. "Georgia on My Mind" (H. Carmichael/S. Gorrell), original form

In the reharmonization, the A–7 target chord is approached by its dominant, E7, which is a perfect fifth above A–7. To create the new progression, I work backwards from E7 using dominant seventh chords a perfect fifth apart.

Note the error in the melody/harmony combinations. E7 with G in the lead produces a ♯9 melody/harmony combination. While ♯9 is an available note on E7, it has a tendency to resolve down. In its current location, it is moving up. In the example below, a melody/harmony error is indicated with an "x". Play the phrase and evaluate the blend of melody notes and chord tones. How does it sound to you?

Fig. 3.6. "Georgia on My Mind," with extended dominants and melody/harmony error

To clear up this melody/harmony combination, the next example uses a tritone substitution, Bb7 for E7. Using this Bb7 chord to correct the melody/harmony clash is an option—play the phrase, listen, and decide which sounds best to you.

Fig. 3.7. "Georgia on My Mind," melody/harmony error corrected using tritone substitution

Any chord placed between two dominant chords may be described as **interpolated**. This new chord briefly delays resolution. Commonly, the interpolated chord is a minor seventh chord placed between two dominants in a pattern. In the examples that follow, the A–7 is an interpolated chord.

Sometimes, you may choose to ignore a single interpolated or interrupting chord when reharmonizing with extended dominant chords. In fig. 3.8, the A–7 chord was skipped over, and extended dominants were added before it. Working backward by perfect fifth root (extended dominant) motion from D7 yields A7, E7, B7, and F#7.

Fig. 3.8. "Georgia on My Mind," with an interpolated chord delaying resolution between A7 and D7

Analyzing each melody/harmony combination reveals one error: an 11 in the lead of E7, which creates an unwanted b9 interval against the third of the chord.

Fig. 3.9. "Georgia on My Mind," 11 in the lead

This melody/harmony error can be corrected by adding the suspended fourth (sus4) to the E7 chord.

Fig. 3.10. "Georgia on My Mind," melody/harmony error corrected

In the next example, F7 substitutes for B7 on beat 2 of the second measure. Listen to the effect of this tritone substitution on the melody/harmony relationship.

Fig. 3.11. "Georgia on My Mind," with tritone substitution

Another variation of the extended dominant/tritone substitution technique is shown below. D7 is the target chord. It is approached, working backward, with two extended dominant chords. Chords appear only on strong beats, 1 and 3, of the second measure in order to maintain the extended dominant sound while reducing the number of chords per bar. Reducing the number of chords in each bar will help to produce a smoother sound, and is particularly desirable if the performance tempo is medium to fast.

Fig. 3.12. "Georgia on My Mind," variation: extended dominant/tritone substitution

Analyze the melody/harmony relationships in measure 2. The B♭ quarter note (♭5) moving up against E7 may be too harsh in this context.

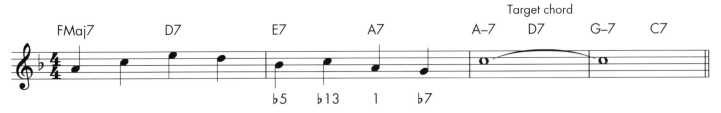

Fig. 3.13. "Georgia on My Mind," with ♭5 melody/harmony relationship

The next example uses Bb7 (tritone substitution for E7) to smooth out this melody/harmony combination.

Fig. 3.14. "Georgia on My Mind," corrected with tritone substitution

Thinking of Bb7 as a new target allows for further variation. Working backwards from this new target, locate its dominant, F7, and its secondary dominant, C7. The melody/harmony combinations are correct, but the increasing number of chords in the phrase may result in an overly active harmonic rhythm. This phrase will sound very busy, especially at fast performance tempos.

Fig. 3.15. "Georgia on My Mind," with active harmonic rhythm

More variations of these patterns may be found by converting dominant chords that fall on strong beats to minor seventh chords. This yields a slightly smoother texture.

The phrase below is a good candidate for variation of this kind. (Beats 1 and 3 in 4/4 are considered rhythmically stronger than beats 2 and 4.)

Fig. 3.16. "Georgia on My Mind," reharmonized with extended dominant sevenths only

Below, F#7 is converted to C–7, and E7sus4 is converted to E–7. Listen to and compare the two examples. Note in the following example that the minor seventh chords are always placed on strong beats.

Fig. 3.17. "Georgia on My Mind," reharmonized using a combination of extended dominants and minor seventh chords

EXTENDED II-V7 PATTERNS

Patterns that move from minor seventh to dominant seventh with roots a fourth apart, or minor seventh to dominant seventh with roots that move down by half step, are called II-V7 patterns. If they are produced as a variation of extended dominants, they are called extended II-V7 patterns.

The progression below is a good candidate for the conversion of extended dominants to II-V7 patterns because the melody will not create unwanted ♭9 or unwanted tritone interval combinations with the converted chords.

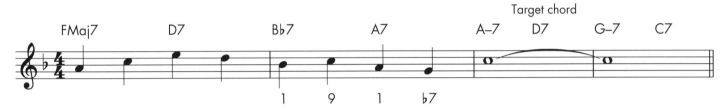

Fig. 3.18. "Georgia on My Mind," original form

The B♭7 at the beginning of measure 2 has now been converted to B♭–7. Its minor seventh quality adds variety to the extended dominant chain. The progression in measures 2–4 is an example of an extended II-V7 pattern.

Fig. 3.19. "Georgia on My Mind," reharmonized using extended II-V7 patterns

EXERCISES

Reharmonize these phrases using extended dominants or extended II-V7 combinations. Select a variety of target chords and approach each differently. Carefully analyze melody/harmony combinations and use tritone substitution to fix poor combinations. Check your reharmonizations against the reference examples at the end of this book to see if you're on the right track.

EXERCISE 3.1

Original form:

Your reharmonization:

EXERCISE 3.2

Original form:

Your reharmonization 1:

Your reharmonization 2:

Notice that these melodies consist mainly of quarter notes, dotted quarter notes, or half notes. The extended dominant or extended II-V7 technique works best with melodic rhythms of this sort. With only one or two melody notes per chord, you can quickly solve melody/harmony clashes with tritone substitutions.

EXERCISE 3.3

Original form:

Your reharmonization 1:

Your reharmonization 2:

EXERCISE 3.4

Original form:

Your reharmonization 1:

Your reharmonization 2:

DISPLACEMENT

Displacement changes the shape of a harmonic progression by moving a target chord to a point later in the progression. This chord movement maintains emphasis on the target chord, but stretches the overall shape of the progression by shifting the locations of harmonic cadences.

Displacing a target chord creates an open space within the phrase. That open space can then be filled with new chord changes. If a target chord is displaced by only a beat or two, the reharmonization will be similar to the original phrase. Displacement of more than a measure will create a more dramatic change.

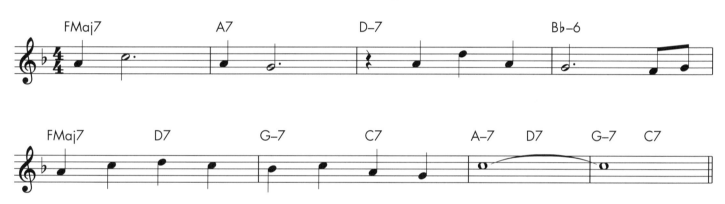

Fig. 4.1. "Georgia on My Mind," original form

In the reharmonization, the A7 in measure 2 and the Bb–6 in measure 4 is displaced. The open space created by the displacement is filled by a II-V7 pattern in measure 2, and by using Bb6 before Bb–6 in measure 4.

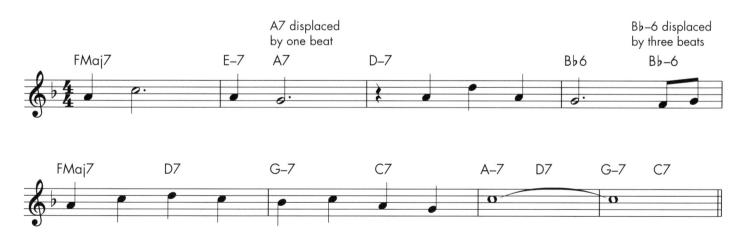

Fig. 4.2. "Georgia on My Mind," with displacement

A cadential dominant chord is often a good choice as a displaced target chord. Dominant seventh chords have usually been carefully placed in order to establish the framework of the original phrase. Displacing these chords produces a noticeable change in the harmonic shape.

There are several ways to approach displaced dominant chords. They are often paired with related II–7s, forming a II-V7 pattern. They may also be preceded by another dominant chord a perfect fifth or a half step higher. A displaced target chord may also be approached using any of the other techniques discussed throughout this book.

Fig. 4.3. "My Ship" (K. Weill/I. Gershwin), original form

Fig. 4.4. "My Ship," with displaced dominant seventh and related II–7 chords

The next example shows reharmonization using displacement of G7 and C7. The displaced dominants are then preceded by extended dominants. Note the melody/harmony clashes. Look closely at the melody/harmony relationships, and note where tritone substitution (dominant chords a tritone higher) could be used to fix melody/harmony clashes.

A melody/harmony clash is found on beat 2 of measure 1. The F♮ melody note forms an unwanted ♭9 interval with chord tone E.

A melody/harmony clash is also found on beat 4. The A♮ melody note forms an unwanted ♭9 interval with chord tone G♯.

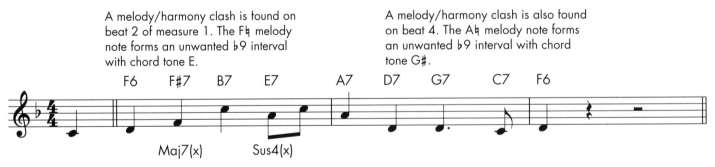

Fig. 4.5. "My Ship," with displacement and melody/harmony clashes

To fix the melody/harmony problem found in measure 1, beat 2, I do two things. I use tritone substitution to change F#7 to C7, and adjust the chord quality to sus4 to account for the fourth in the melody.

To fix the melody/harmony problem found in measure 1, beat 4, I adjust the chord quality to sus4 to account for the fourth in the melody.

Fig. 4.6. "My Ship," melody/harmony clashes fixed

Fig. 4.7. "My Ship," variation replacing A7 in measure 2 with its tritone substitution (Eb7)

Fig. 4.8. "My Ship," variation replacing B7 in measure 1 with its tritone substitution (F7)

Fig. 4.9. "My Ship," variation leading to target chord (C7) using extended dominants and their tritone substitutions

Notice in the example above that the resolution of Eb7(#11) in measure 1 to D7 in measure 2 is delayed by the interrupting A7 chord.

SPECIAL CASES

Two examples of displacement deserve special mention.

1. A minor seventh chord with ♭3 in the lead may be displaced by a II-V7 pattern a half step higher. The melody note that was originally ♭3 becomes tension 9 on the II–7 of the newly inserted pattern.

2. A minor seventh chord with ♭5 in the lead may be displaced by a II-V7 pattern a half step higher. The melody note that was originally ♭5 becomes tension 11 on the II–7 of the newly inserted pattern.

DISPLACEMENT WITH ♭3 IN THE LEAD OF MINOR SEVENTH CHORDS

You can use displacement of a minor seventh with a ♭3 lead in songs such as "The Song Is You" and "Like Someone in Love." Notice the melody/harmony relationship in bar 2 of "The Song Is You."

Fig. 4.10. "The Song Is You" (J. Kern/O. Hammerstein), original form

Fig. 4.11. "The Song Is You," D–7 displaced and preceded by a II-V7 pattern a half step higher

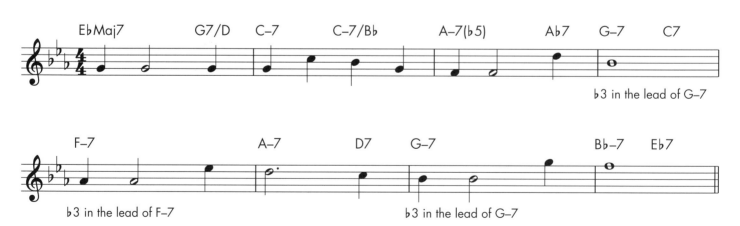

Fig. 4.12. "Like Someone in Love" (J. Van Heusen/J. Burke), original form

In the reharmonization, each ♭3 melody note becomes a tension 9 over a new II-V pattern.

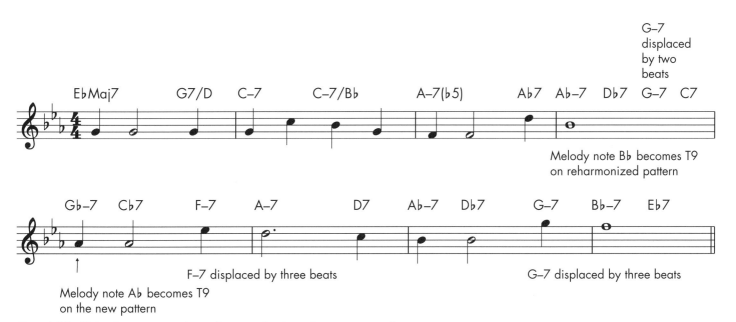

Fig. 4.13. "Like Someone in Love," using displaced minor sevenths

DISPLACEMENT WITH ♭5 IN THE LEAD OF MINOR SEVENTH CHORDS

Displacement of minor7(♭5) chords with a ♭5 lead is found in songs such as "Stella by Starlight" and "Rising Tide." Notice the melody/harmony relationship in bar 1 of the example below.

This technique works well wherever ♭5 is found in the lead of a minor 7(♭5) chord. The melody note, which was originally ♭5, becomes tension 11 on the II–7 of the newly inserted pattern.

Fig. 4.14. "Stella by Starlight" (V. Young/N. Washington), original form

Below, C–7(♭5) is displaced and preceded by a II-V7 pattern a half step higher. The melody note G♭ becomes tension 11 on the new pattern.

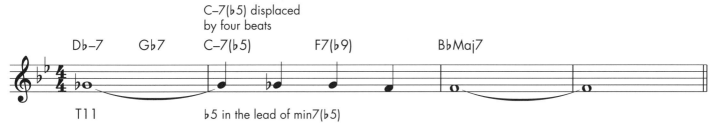

Fig. 4.15. "Stella by Starlight," reharmonized

Fig. 4.16. "Rising Tide" (R. Felts), original form

F#–7(b5) is displaced and preceded by a II-V7 pattern a half step higher. The melody note C becomes tension 11 on the new pattern.

Fig. 4.17. "Rising Tide," reharmonized

EXERCISES

Reharmonize the following examples using displacement, extended dominants, diatonic approach, and simple substitution. Analyze your variations.

EXERCISE 4.1

Original form:

Your reharmonization:

Use displacement to reharmonize the next two examples.

EXERCISE 4.2

Your reharmonization 1:

Your reharmonization 2:

EXERCISE 4.3

Original form:

Your reharmonization 1:

Your reharmonization 2:

5

MODAL INTERCHANGE

Modal interchange (MI) is the practice of borrowing chords from a parallel key—a key or scale that starts on the same pitch as the current key but uses different combinations of whole steps and half steps.

Modal interchange chords vary the color of a diatonic phrase. You can add color to a C major phrase, for example, by reharmonizing with chords derived from one of the common forms of C minor: natural minor (also called Aeolian mode), harmonic minor, melodic minor. Try this exercise:

    1. Write out the ascending forms of the C natural minor scale, the C harmonic minor scale, and the C melodic minor scale.

C natural minor

C harmonic minor

C melodic minor

Fig. 5.1. Write in your scales on the staves above.

    2. Build seventh chords on each pitch of each minor scale.

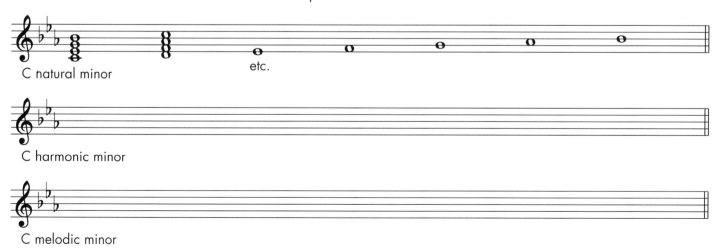

C natural minor

etc.

C harmonic minor

C melodic minor

Fig. 5.2. Write seventh chords on each scale degree.

3. Examine the chord qualities that are found on each step of each scale. For example, the seventh chord built on the first step of the C natural minor scale is a minor seventh, and the chord built on the first step of the C harmonic minor scale is I–(Maj7). Chords created from parallel scales may substitute for each other, melody permitting.

Twelve commonly used modal interchange choices are listed below. They are described both with Roman numerals and with chord symbols in the key of C, but are proportionally the same in any key.

In this example, the twelve chord choices may be inserted into progressions that had originally been in the key of C major. All of these borrowed chords are nondiatonic, but are related to the original key. Composers and musicians have historically referred to these borrowed minor chords as "darker" variations of the original major-key chord qualities. Memorize the Roman numeral and chord quality for the MI chords, and try naming them in all twelve keys.

Twelve Common Modal Interchange Chords				
These chords may substitute for each other, melody permitting.				
Original Diatonic Chord in C Major	MI Chord	Roman Numeral for MI Chord	Modal Source for MI Chord	Available Tensions for MI Chord
CMaj7	C–7	I–7	Aeolian (natural) minor	9, 11
CMaj7	C–6	I–6	melodic minor	Maj7, 9, 11
CMaj7	C–(Maj7)	I–(Maj7)	melodic or harmonic minor	9, 11, 13
D–7	D–7(♭5)	II–7(♭5)	Aeolian or harmonic minor	9, 11, ♭13
D–7	D♭Maj7	♭IIMaj7	Phrygian	9, ♯11, 13
E–7	E♭Maj7	♭IIIMaj7	Aeolian minor	9, ♯11, 13
FMaj7	F–6	IV–6	Aeolian or harmonic minor	Maj7, 9, 11
FMaj7	F–7	IV–7	Aeolian or harmonic minor	9, 11
G7	G7(♭9)	V7(♭9)	harmonic minor	♭9, ♭13 (♯9 optional)
G7	G–7	V–7	Aeolian minor	9, 11
A–7	A♭Maj7	♭VIMaj7	Aeolian or harmonic minor	9, ♯11, 13
B°7	B♭7	♭VII7	Aeolian minor	9, ♯11, 13

Fig. 5.3. "Never on Sunday" (M. Hadjidakis/B. Towne), original form

In the example below, the modal interchange chord I–6 is used to **vary the color** of the original I6. Note that in the last bar, G–7 is not available as a variation of G7, since the melody note is a major third above the root. A ♭9 clash would be produced between B in the melody and B♭ in the supporting chord.

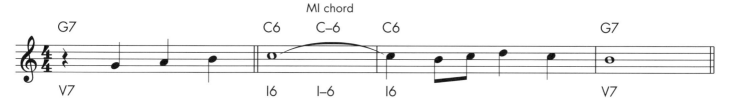

Fig. 5.4. "Never on Sunday," reharmonized with a modal interchange chord

This practice, alternating I6 with I–6, will not work if the original melody has a major third above the root in the lead. Combining a minor chord with a major third in the melody produces an unwanted ♭9 interval between the two pitches.

LINKING DIATONIC CHORDS WITH MODAL INTERCHANGE CHORDS

Modal interchange chords may also be used as a **link between two diatonic chords.** Think of the second diatonic chord as a target and lead to it using a modal interchange chord that has strong root motion into the target.

In fig. 5.5, the target chord G7 is approached by F–6. The root motion is strong. (Remember from chapter 2 that strong root motion occurs when the approach chord and the target chord are not a diatonic third or sixth apart.) Strong root motion guarantees a strong contrast between the approach chord and the target chord, resulting in a strong cadence. Use of strong cadences is typical when reharmonizing phrases with modal interchange chords. Strong root motion ensures that each successive chord in the series introduces at least two new chord tones. New chord tones make the reharmonization more interesting to the listener.

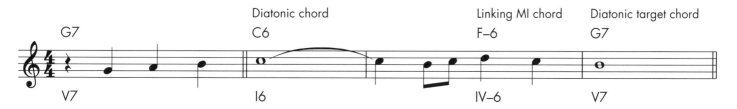

Fig. 5.5. "Never on Sunday," with a modal interchange chord as a link between diatonic chords

MOVEMENT AMONG MODAL INTERCHANGE CHORDS

A modal interchange chord may move to another modal interchange chord before returning to a diatonic chord. The root motion between neighboring modal interchange chords is usually strong.

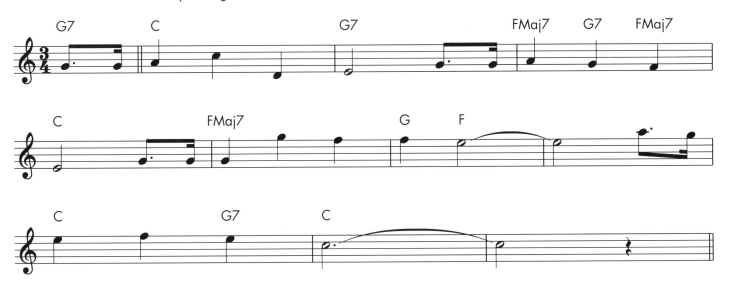

Fig. 5.6. Original form

The final reharmonized cadence below uses modal interchange chords. These chords lead with strong root motion to a diatonic target chord.

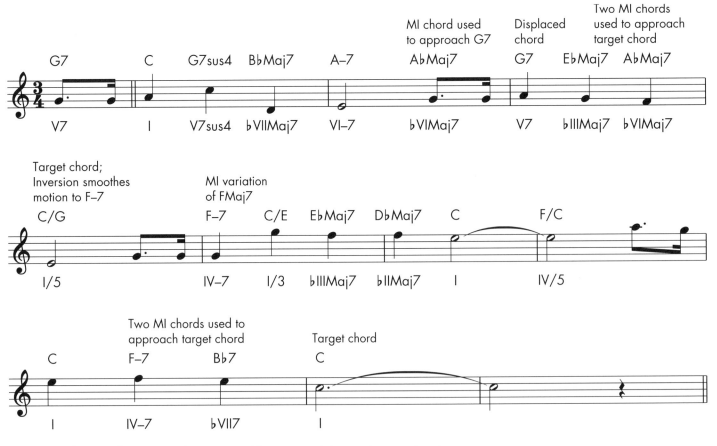

Fig. 5.7. Phrase reharmonized using neighboring modal interchange chords

To maintain the basic tonality of the phrase, be careful not to overdo chord borrowing. Using more than three modal interchange chords in a row can create a key change or an ambiguous tonal center. Unless you specifically desire this more radical effect, limit yourself to three modal interchange chords before returning to a diatonic chord. This will maintain a clear tonal center while adding new color.

REPLACING DIATONIC CHORDS WITH MODAL INTERCHANGE CHORDS

A modal interchange chord may be used to completely replace the original chord in a phrase. The modal interchange chord does not have to serve the same function (tonic, subdominant, or dominant) as the original chord, since the goal of modal interchange is to expand the harmonic color of the phrase. Maintaining similar harmonic function for each of the original chords (i.e., using simple substitution) remains a viable option, but results in a less colorful reharmonization.

Fig. 5.8. "Georgia on My Mind," original form

In the reharmonization below, modal interchange chords replace the original chords in measures 2, 3, and 4.

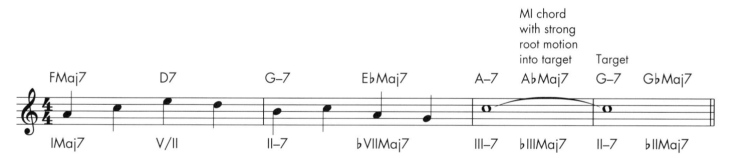

Fig. 5.9. "Georgia on My Mind," with modal interchange chords

In Fig. 5.10, I use a variety of reharmonization techniques. Look for displacement, tritone substitution, and modal interchange. Also, note the strong motion between MI chords in the measures 3 and 4.

Fig. 5.10. "Georgia on My Mind," with several reharmonization techniques

EXERCISES

Reharmonize the following examples. Use modal interchange chords and other techniques as you see fit. Then, do a Roman numeral analysis of your variations. Remember that choosing target chords and using displacement techniques are often good starting points. Check melody/harmony relationships carefully.

EXERCISE 5.1

Original form:

Your reharmonization 1:

Your reharmonization 2:

EXERCISE 5.2

Original form:

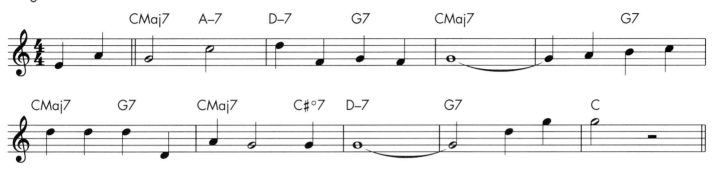

Your reharmonization 1:

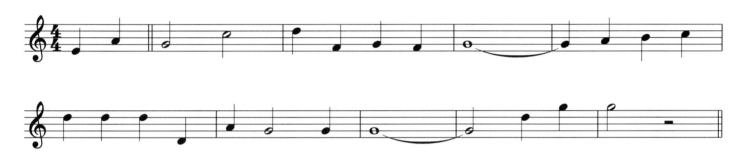

Your reharmonization 2:

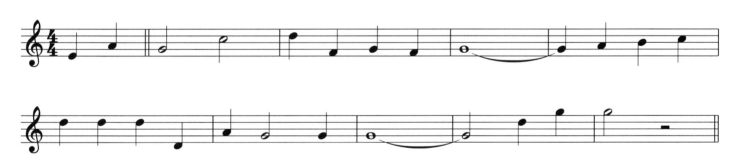

EXERCISE 5.3

Original form:

Your reharmonization 1:

Your reharmonization 2:

Your reharmonization 3:

REHARMONIZATION
USING BASS LINES

Sometimes the best way to build is from the ground up. Musically speaking, one might start by creating counterpoint between a bass line and a melody. Writing a new bass line for an existing melody can suggest new reharmonization possibilities. From this bass line, you can derive various cadence choices, including extended dominants and modal interchange chords, to complete the reharmonization.

Fig. 6.1. Original form

Reharmonizing basic folk, rock, pop, and classical styles normally requires a clear tonal center. In these styles the bass line should be diatonic to the key or move chromatically to a diatonic pitch.

In a typical case, the bass line will form a stepwise descending counterline into a target chord.

Fig. 6.2. The bass line creates strong root motion to B♭Maj7

Bass lines usually move toward target chords with strong, stepwise root motion. Chords built upon these notes will have a strong cadential flow, and will sound most effective at phrase endings.

Fig. 6.3. Bass line resolution by step (strong root motion)

When composing a bass line, you may move forward into the target or move backward from it.

To move backward from a target chord:

1. Identify a target chord.

2. Choose a bass note directly before the target chord that approaches the target with strong root motion.

3. Create a stepwise line of bass notes that move either up or down into the cadential note.

To move forward to a target chord:

1. Identify a target chord.

2. Lead forward into this target chord using a stepwise series of notes that approach it from either above or below.

Be sure to move your bass lines consistently up or down into the target chord. Failure to maintain a consistent direction will weaken the cadential possibilities of the chord progressions derived from the bass line.

Also, consider the interval combinations between the melody and the bass line. If you desire a smooth reharmonization, avoid more than three consecutive dissonant intervals between the bass line and the melody. (In this context, dissonant intervals are seconds, fourths, fifths, and sevenths. Minor sevenths, major seconds, and augmented fourths/diminished fifths are the most dissonant combinations.)

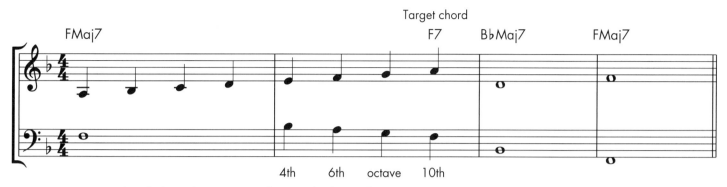

Fig. 6.4. Bass and melody with a variety of interval relationships

Think of the bass notes as chord tones 1, 3, 5, or 7 of potential reharmonized chord changes. Thinking of these notes as 9, 11, or 13 will produce hybrid chord voicings (see chapter 14) or may produce chord symbols that are overly complex (see chapter 7).

Fig. 6.5. An effective reharmonization using the bass notes from fig. 6.4

Be cautious about using chord tone 7 in the bass (third inversion), unless a root position form of the same chord is used directly before the inversion.

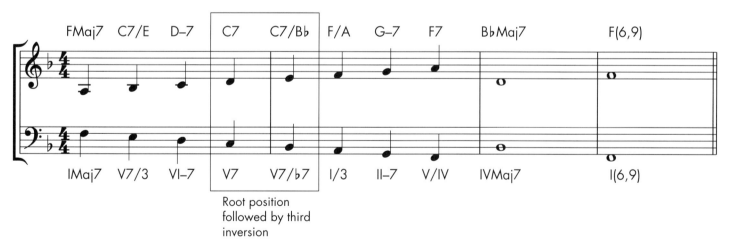

Fig. 6.6. Third-inversion C7 chord following C7 in root position

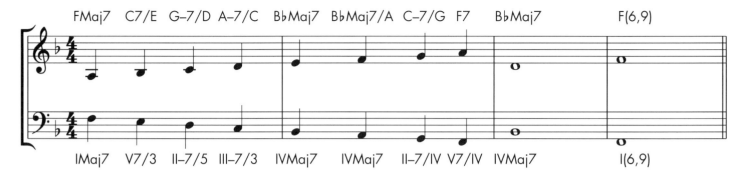

Fig. 6.7. Third-inversion B♭Maj7 chord following B♭maj7 in root position

If the chords are not in this sequence, the chord structure with the 7 in the bass will often sound like an incomplete voicing of the bass note. For example: C7 with a B♭ in the bass (symbol: C/B♭) will be heard as a type of B♭ chord with tensions 9, ♯11, and 13, unless it has a C7 before it to establish context.

These incomplete, ambiguous voicings are called **hybrid chords**. They have a distinctive sound and texture, and should be used carefully. If used indiscriminately, hybrids can break up the sonic texture and mood of a phrase. (Reharmonization examples using hybrid chords in appropriate contexts will be discussed in chapter 14.)

Remember the rule: Keep it simple. When working with busy harmonic rhythms in which there are two, three, or four chords per measure, relatively simple tonal progressions work best.

Fig. 6.8. "Camptown Races" (S. Foster), original form

In the following reharmonization of "Camptown Races," notice the descending stepwise line leading into the D7 target chord. D7 in turn forms a strong cadence to G–7. Each chord in the descending line is either a diatonic chord, a secondary dominant, or a subV7 (tritone substitution for a secondary or primary dominant). The E♭7 is a modal interchange chord that resolves deceptively. It sounds like a ♭VII7 chord in the phrase. ♭VII7 normally resolves to IMaj7, but in this case it moves down by half step to D7.

Fig. 6.9. "Camptown Races," reharmonized using bass line technique

The next two reharmonizations of "Camptown Races" employ less active harmonic rhythms by using mostly half notes in the descending stepwise bass lines.

Fig. 6.10. "Camptown Races," reharmonized using bass line technique

Here's another example:

Fig. 6.11. "Over the Rainbow" (H. Arlen/E.Y. Harburg), reharmonized using bass line technique

Think of the first bass line as a rough draft, and subsequent versions as continuing drafts on the way to the final reharmonization of the phrase. Here is a general step-by-step method for bass-line reharmonization.

1. Choose a target chord.

2. Create a rough draft bass line. Start with stepwise descending half notes into the target chord.

Fig. 6.12. "Over the Rainbow," rough draft bass line

3. Harmonize the rough draft bass line. Simple diatonic chords often provide a good starting point.

4. Evaluate melody/harmony combinations, root motion, and harmonic rhythm as you proceed.

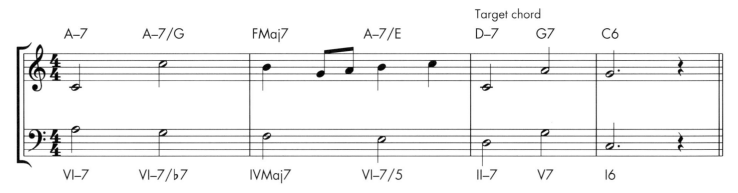

Fig. 6.13. "Over the Rainbow," harmonized bass line

5. Experiment with your bass line by adding chromatic variations to it. For example, note the E♭ bass note added in the example below.

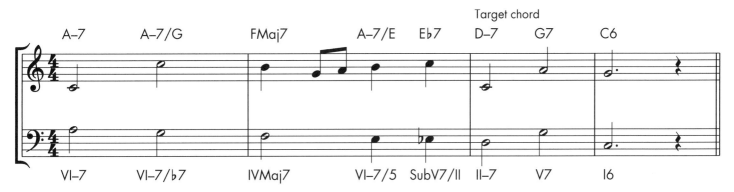

Fig. 6.14. "Over the Rainbow," variation

The example below shows further embellishment to the bass line.

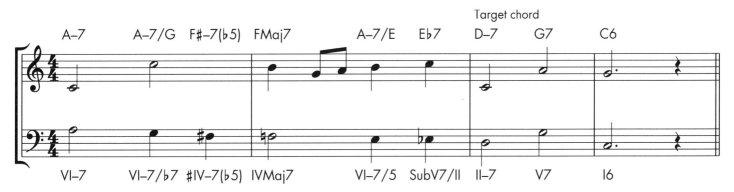

Fig. 6.15. "Over the Rainbow," bass line embellishment

Here is the final variation. Which variation sounds best to you?

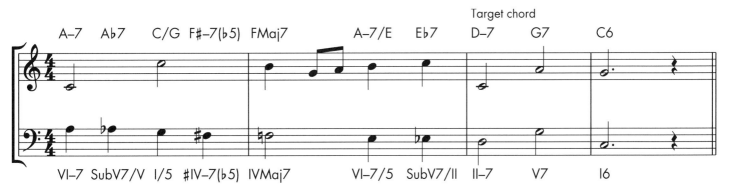

Fig. 6.16. "Over the Rainbow," final variation

The same multi-step process can be used with an ascending bass line. Below is a rough draft ascending line leading by step into the target chord.

Fig. 6.17. Rough draft bass line

Next, I harmonize the rough draft bass line. Simple diatonic chords often are good starting points.

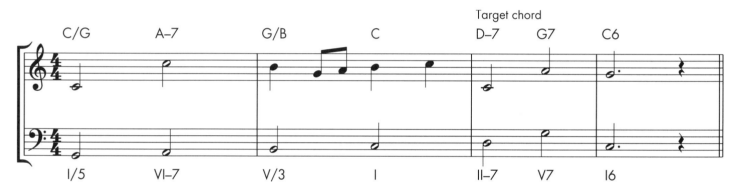

Fig. 6.18. Bass line reharmonized

A further variation using the same ascending bass line:

Fig. 6.19. Bass line, variation

A few subtle changes to the melody line may be used to solve melody/harmony conflicts and to provide color and variety to the reharmonization. This approach works best with melodies that are extremely familiar. It should not be overused. **Melodic variation may be used with all reharmonization techniques, not just bass line technique.**

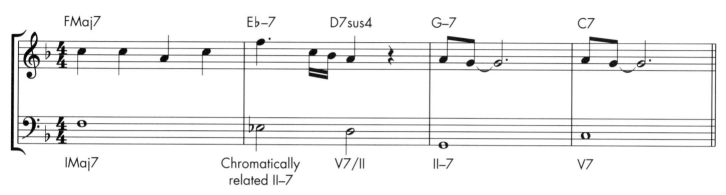

Fig. 6.20. Melody notes changed to allow for chromatic II-V7 pattern

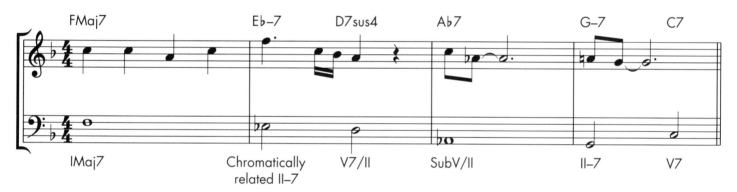

Fig. 6.21. Two melody notes changed in measure 3 to allow for tritone substitution for V7/V

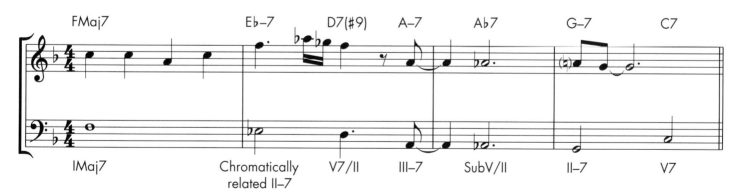

Fig. 6.22. Melody note and melodic rhythm changed to allow for chromatic II-V7 pattern

EXERCISES

Melody and bass line combinations can yield a huge variety of reharmonization choices. In these exercises, experiment with a variety of bass line rhythms. For example, try one example with mostly quarter notes in the bass, the next with half notes, and the last with a mixture of bass note rhythms. Supply a Roman numeral analysis with each reharmonization.

EXERCISE 6.1

Original form:

Your reharmonization 1:

Your reharmonization 2:

Your reharmonization 3:

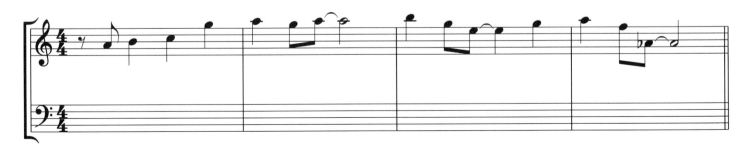

EXERCISE 6.2

Original form:

Your reharmonization 1:

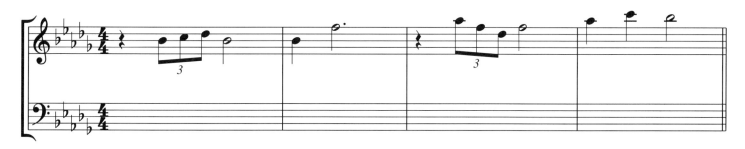

Your reharmonization 2:

Your reharmonization 3:

EXERCISE 6.3

Original form:

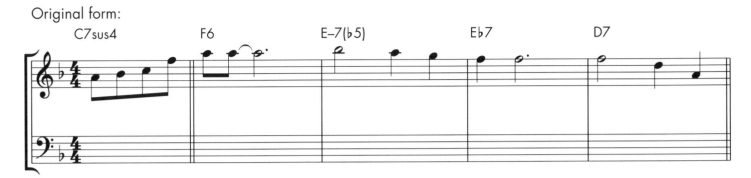

Your reharmonization 1:

Your reharmonization 2:

Your reharmonization 3:

7

CORRECTION OF
FAULTY CHORD SYMBOLS

Chord symbols have both a harmonic, functional meaning and a visual presentation. When reading a chord chart, an experienced musician will be interested in both. In order to keep the meaning and visual presentation of each chord symbol as clear as possible, a composer must understand the meanings of chord symbols in their various forms. Ultimately most composers hope their work will reach a large audience. By taking steps to ensure clarity, a composer can increase the possibility that this will happen.

There are often a number of ways to express a musical idea using chord symbols. If the chord symbols are unclear, the harmonic function may be hidden, and without a clear understanding of the harmonic function, effective reharmonization choices may be overlooked.

The correct presentation of a chord symbol requires knowledge of musical styles. Folk, classic rock, and hymn tunes use a mostly triadic vocabulary, so chord symbols used in presenting music in these idioms should be almost exclusively triadic.

On the other hand, jazz, contemporary film music, many fusion styles, and jazz-influenced world music styles demand seventh chords. The seventh chords express the necessary pitches contained in the harmony, and give the theory-trained musician further information about the harmonic intent of the composer.

The example below is a typical presentation of IV6, V7, and IMaj7 in the key of G major. The subdominant (SD) chord written in this form (C6) is common practice in folk, country, or pop styles, but is less common in jazz standards.

Fig. 7.1. Typical chord symbol presentation, pop forms

Jazz standards, with their numerous examples of II-V7 patterns, commonly include chord symbols such as those shown in the example below. The C6 and A–7 chords include all of the same notes. The symbols for the chords account for the notes in the voicing, but send different stylistic messages.

Fig. 7.2. Typical chord symbol presentation, jazz style

In Fig. 7.3, the use of triads is inappropriate and stylistically incorrect. The standard tune style is not presented clearly by triadic chord symbols. Standard jazz chord symbols usually include additional pitches—such as sevenths.

Fig. 7.3. "Misty," with inappropriate chord symbols

Changing the chord symbols to seventh chords brings their representation into sync with the normal chord vocabulary of jazz standards. The use of major seventh chord symbols on E♭ and A♭ makes the chords easier to analyze as IMaj7 and IVMaj7. Using sevenths on B♭ minor and E♭ makes the chords easier to analyze as V/IV and the related II–7 of V/IV.

Fig. 7.4. Appropriate chord symbols indicate necessary pitches and clarify the harmonic function of each chord.

The example below is incorrect. Tensions 9 and 13 are diatonic to the key and are automatically implied in a standard tune style. Because diatonic tensions are part of jazz style, it would be considered overkill to write them out explicitly. Often, when a writer includes diatonic tensions in the chord symbol, he or she really is suggesting a specific chord voicing without writing it out in notation.

Fig. 7.5. Incorrect chord symbols: Diatonic tensions need not be written

The next example shows a clearer way to write chord symbols and indicate specific voicings. As shown here, you may need to use both bass and treble clefs to create voicings over a wider range. (Piano voicings are discussed in chapter 10.)

Fig. 7.6. Correct chord symbols: Diatonic tensions that are implied are not included in the chord symbols

While diatonic tensions are implied in standard jazz style, **all nondiatonic tensions** should be included in the chord symbols.

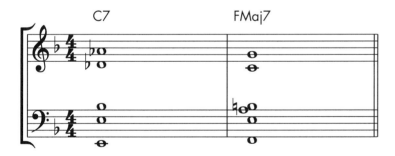

Fig. 7.7. Incorrect chord symbols: Nondiatonic tensions should be indicated

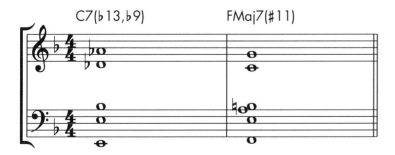

Fig. 7.8. Correct chord symbols: Nondiatonic tensions are included

Another common chord symbol notation error is to mix chord symbols derived from sharp keys and flat keys within the same short phrase. It is visually confusing, and will make it much harder for the musicians to read and perform the music correctly.

Fig. 7.9. Incorrect notation: Symbols are mixed from sharp and flat key areas

Fig. 7.10. Correct notation: All symbols are from sharp key area

Avoid the word "add" in chord symbols. Tension 11 is mislabeled this way most often.

Fig. 7.11. Incorrect notation: Diatonic tensions are written explicitly

Since tension 11 is diatonic to the key, the combination of chord symbol and notation shown in this example is a clearer representation.

Fig. 7.12. Correct notation: Diatonic tensions that are implied are not included in the chord symbol

Diminished seventh chords represent a special problem. Any diminished seventh can be expressed as a series of four enharmonically equal chord symbols. The chords below share the same chord tones. However, context will determine which chord symbol best represents the sound and harmonic function of the chord.

Fig. 7.13. Diminished seventh chords, enharmonic spelling

Notation can make a chord's function in a progression difficult to understand. In the example, the **pitches** in E°7 are correct, but the chord's dominant function leading to D–7 is not clearly shown. The notes E, G, B♭, and D♭ make the sound of a dominant resolution to D–7, but it is difficult to see this relationship if the chord symbol E°7 is used to describe these pitches. (For more information on the functions of diminished chords, see chapter 12.)

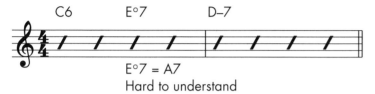

E°7 = A7
Hard to understand

Fig. 7.14. Confusing diminished chord symbol

C♯°7, on the other hand, contains all the tones of A7, the dominant of D minor, without the root. Using C♯°7 to represent these pitches makes the dominant resolution between these two chords much easier to grasp.

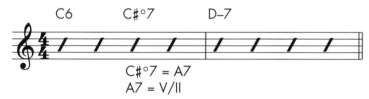

C♯°7 = A7
A7 = V/II

Fig. 7.15. Clarified diminished chord symbol

The progression below is overly complex. First, it represents a line cliché as a series of separate chords, and second, it contains a diminished seventh chord whose dominant function is not clearly expressed. (A line cliché is a stepwise descending or ascending line that moves against a single stationary chord. Chapter 11 covers the use of line clichés as a reharmonization technique.)

Fig. 7.16. Overly complex notation

A line cliché is most clearly represented as a single chord with a line moving against it. Diminished seventh chords normally resolve by half-step root motion. Two clues that a line cliché is hidden in the progression are:

1. Presence of a secondary dominant chord with an augmented quality

2. Presence of a diminished seventh that does not resolve by step

In fig. 7.16, a chromatic line moving over a C triad is written as three separate chords. This chord progression is overly complex and hides the tonic (T) function of the C triad. Also, G°7 has a dominant sound approaching F6, but the dominant relationship is not clearly expressed by the chord symbol.

The corrected form of the progression is shown below:

Fig. 7.17. Notation, corrected

The next figure shows another example of overly complex chord symbols that hide the harmonic function of the phrase.

Fig. 7.18. Complex chord symbol notation

To simplify and clarify the chord symbols, use Cmaj7 and G7sus4. They represent the same vertical pitches as in the example above, but are expressed in a way that clearly reveals their harmonic function.

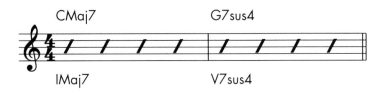

Fig. 7.19. Notation, corrected

Complex chord symbols like E–7/C or D–7/G may sometimes be clear and functionally accurate if they show true hybrid chord function or if they are part of a progression over a sustained note—a **pedal tone**.

(A pedal tone is a single note sustained above, below, or through a changing chord pattern. Since it is usually sustained for several bars, using a series of chord symbols over the same bass note is a clear and harmonically correct way to show that a pedal tone is being used. Hybrid chords and the use of pedal tones are presented in chapter 14.)

EXERCISES

Each of the examples below contains chord symbol errors. Rewrite the chord symbols in correct form on the lower stave, and do a Roman numeral analysis of the progressions.

EXERCISE 7.1

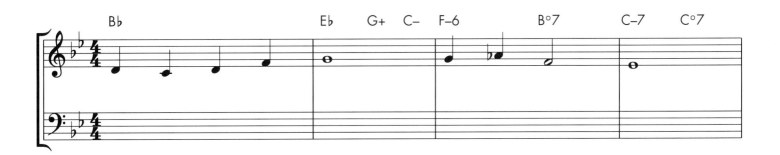

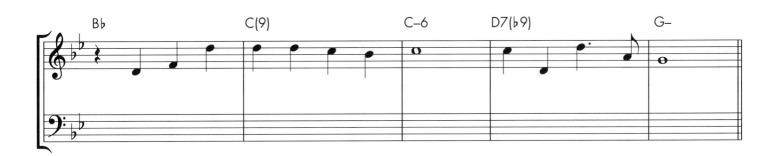

EXERCISE 7.2

Original example:

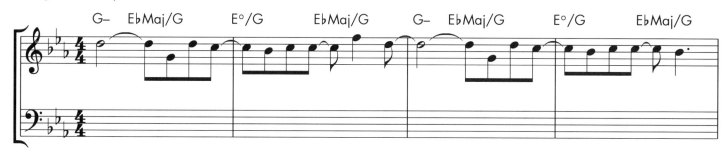

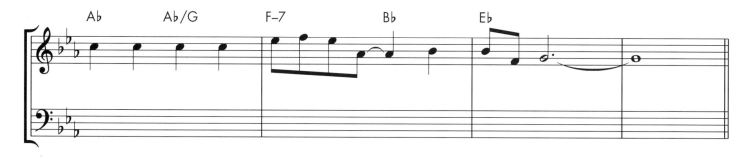

EXERCISE 7.3

"There! I've Said It Again" (D. Mann/R. Evans)

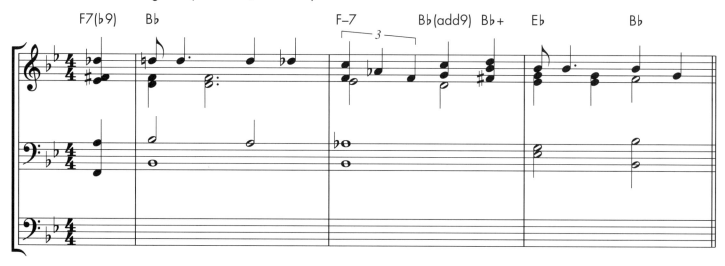

TURNAROUNDS

One important stylistic convention of harmony in jazz and pop standards is that tunes tend to include chords with a tonic, resting function at the beginning and end of the last phrase. If the song form is repeated several times, the listener will hear three or four bars of the same chord and a weak cadence each time the song form is repeated.

Since the key is often established in the first two measures, arrangers have most often reharmonized the last two bars of the musical phrase. These "end of phrase" reharmonizations are called **turnarounds**. New chords placed in these measures provide the necessary harmonic energy to lead into the next phrase.

Turnarounds are used to increase the sense of harmonic motion toward a target chord at the beginning of a new phrase. A turnaround typically consists of four chords, each with a two-beat harmonic rhythm. In a standard 32-bar tune, the turnaround is typically contained in bars 31 and 32. Turnarounds are also often used at the end of an A section in an AABA song form to either increase the cadential energy back to the beginning of the A section or to push the phrase forward to the start of the B section.

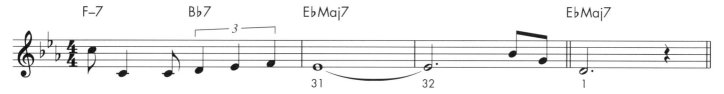

Fig. 8.1. "Misty" (E. Garner), original form

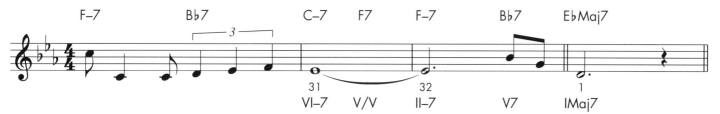

Fig. 8.2. "Misty," reharmonized with a turnaround

Turnarounds are reharmonized within the existing song form. The turnaround is often specifically designed to replace the long IMaj7 chord found in measures 31 and 32 of many jazz standards.

Fig. 8.3. "My Foolish Heart" (N. Washington/V. Young), original form

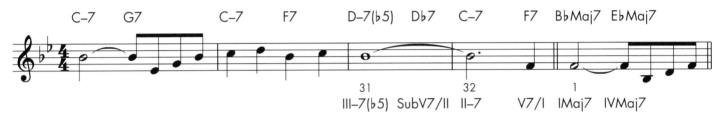

Fig. 8.4. "My Foolish Heart," reharmonized with a turnaround

An arranger or composer may rewrite an existing turnaround to give the tune a personal flavor. Another turnaround is shown below:

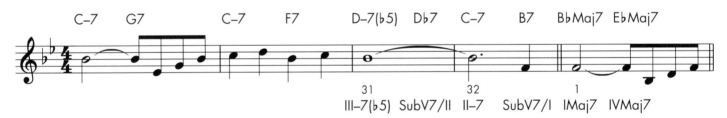

Fig. 8.5. "My Foolish Heart," with new turnaround

This example shows the form of a typical turnaround.

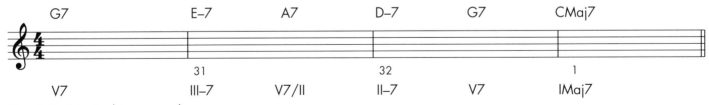

Fig. 8.6. A typical turnaround

The first chord of a turnaround (measure 31) can be any chord that supports the melodic line, but is often a chord with tonic function. The second chord of a typical turnaround (measure 31, beat 3) is a chord that connects forward to one of the chords in measure 32. Think of the chords in measure 32 as target chords. The second chord of the turnaround resolves by strong root motion into one of the targets. It forms a link between the first and third or fourth chords in the turnaround.

The third chord of a typical turnaround (measure 32, beat 1) is a chord that has a subdominant function (SD) and leads by strong root motion into the last chord of the turnaround.

The fourth and usually last chord of a typical turnaround (measure 32, beat 3) is a chord that has dominant function and leads by strong root motion into the first chord of the new phrase.

The examples below illustrate the principles of turnaround construction.

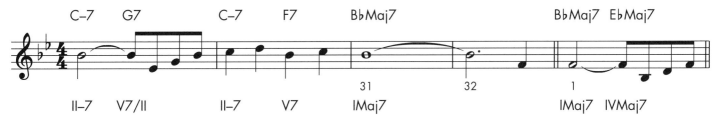

Fig. 8.7. "My Foolish Heart," original form

Note the strong root motion and good melody/harmony combinations in the example below.

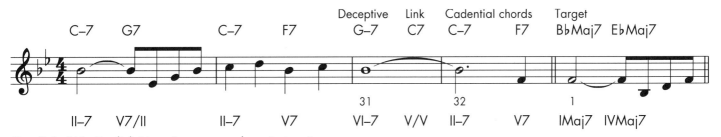

Fig. 8.8. "My Foolish Heart" turnaround: variation 1

The next turnaround uses three chords with strong root motion.

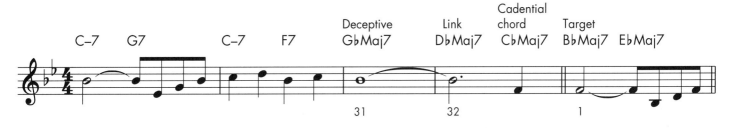

Fig. 8.9. "My Foolish Heart" turnaround: variation 2

In this reharmonization, the turnaround uses only two chords, also with strong root motion.

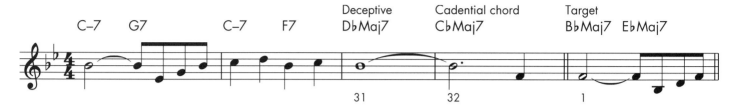

Fig. 8.10. "My Foolish Heart" turnaround: variation 3

The following examples represent typical turnarounds used to lead back to IMaj7. Although the first chord of a turnaround can be *any* chord that makes an acceptable melody/harmony combination, most of the turnarounds here begin with a chord in the tonic family or a chromatic variation of a tonic family chord.

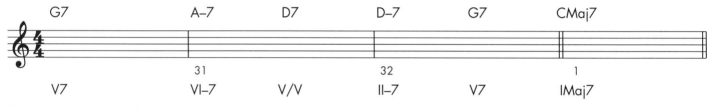

Fig. 8.11. Turnaround: example 1

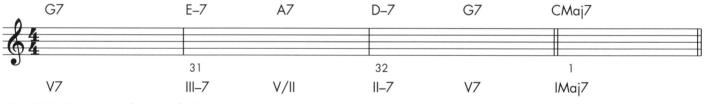

Fig. 8.12. Turnaround: example 2

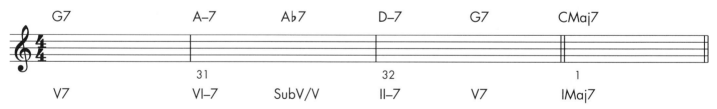

Fig. 8.13. Turnaround: example 3

In the turnaround below in fig. 8.14, the ♭IIIMaj7 chord is a chromatic variation of III–7.

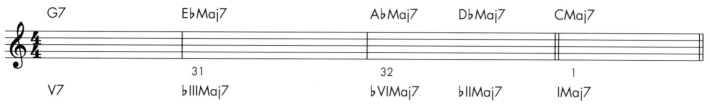

Fig. 8.14. Turnaround: example 4

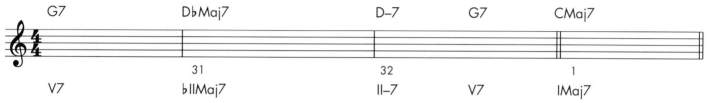

Fig. 8.15. Turnaround: example 5

The examples below show more common turnarounds. Notice that the first chord of the turnaround is often:

- tonic substitution (variations on the III–7 and VI–7)
- modal interchange chord with a root based on III or VI
- IV chord or modal interchange variation of IV (IV–, IV–6, IV–7)
- #IV–7(♭5) chord (a chord that is considered a chromatic variation of IV)
- ♭IIMaj7 (a modal interchange chord that shares many common tones with IV–)
- ♭VIIMaj7 or ♭VII7 (modal interchange chords that share two common tones with IV or IV–)

The turnaround below contains an extra measure. This can be an effective choice in some standard tunes with longer forms.

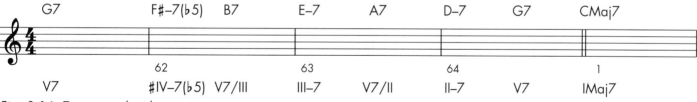

Fig. 8.16. Turnaround with an extra measure

Here are some more advanced turnaround variations:

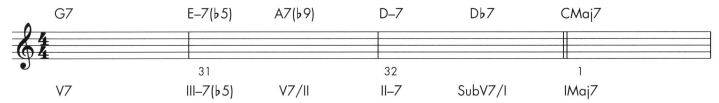

Fig. 8.17. Advanced turnaround: variation 1

Fig. 8.18. Advanced turnaround: variation 2

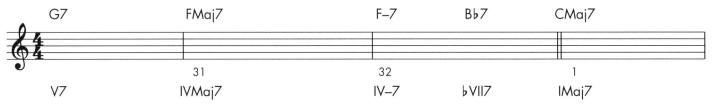

Fig. 8.19. Advanced turnaround: variation 3

The examples below show more typical turnaround combinations.

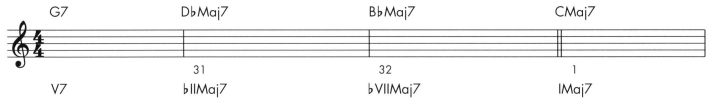

Fig. 8.20. Turnaround: variation 1

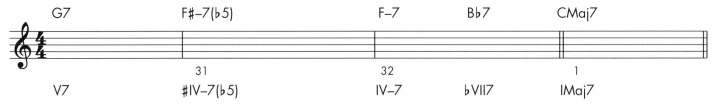

Fig. 8.21. Turnaround: variation 2

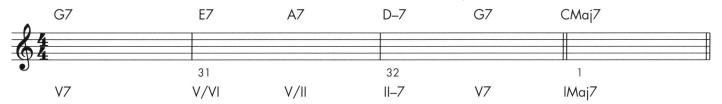

Fig. 8.22. Turnaround: variation 3

The last two examples use A7 (V/II) as the first chord of a turnaround. You may think of the "A" root of the chord as VI in the key. In this case, it functions as a kind of substitution for IMaj7, since I and VI both have tonic function within any key and may substitute for each other.

Similarly, E7 (V/VI) could be used as the first chord of a turnaround. It is based on a III root. I and III both have tonic function within any key and may substitute for each other.

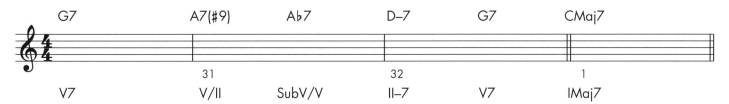

Fig. 8.23. Turnaround: variation 4

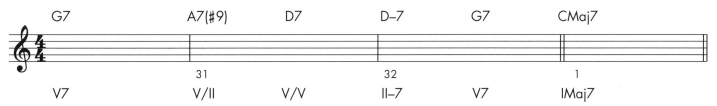

Fig. 8.24. Turnaround: variation 5

EXERCISES

Practice your turnaround technique by reharmonizing the endings of the following
phrases. Work within measures 31 and 32 in each case.

EXERCISE 8.1

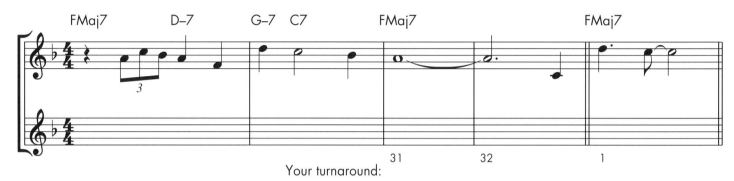

Your turnaround:

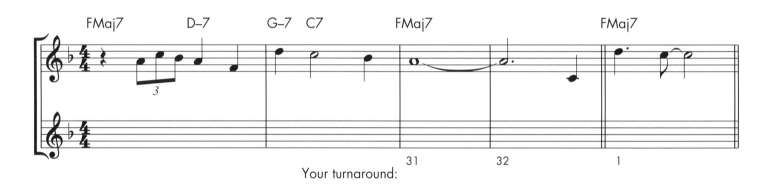

Your turnaround:

EXERCISE 8.2

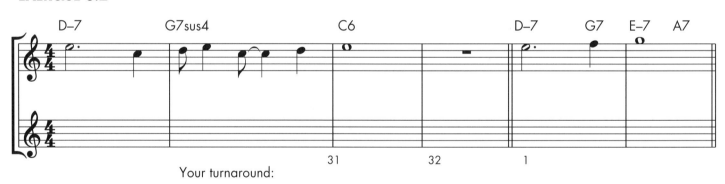

Your turnaround:

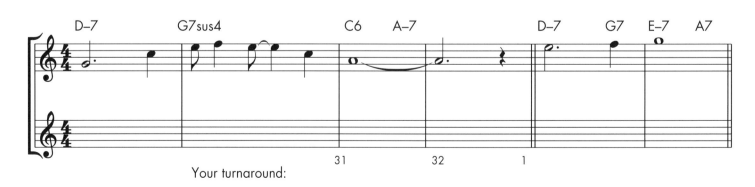

Your turnaround:

EXERCISE 8.3

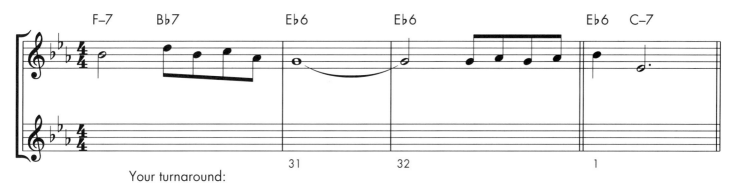

Your turnaround:

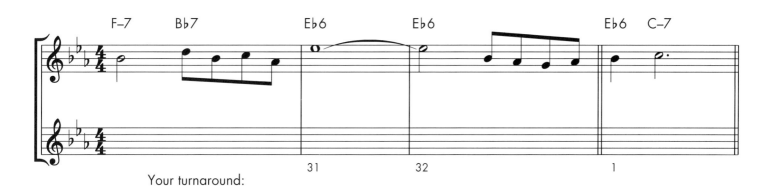

Your turnaround:

TURNAROUNDS THAT LEAD TO A NEW KEY

A similar technique may be used to construct turnarounds that lead to a new key. "Days of Wine and Roses" starts in F major and "turns around" to the key of G major. A transposed melodic pickup note helps make a smooth transition to the new key.

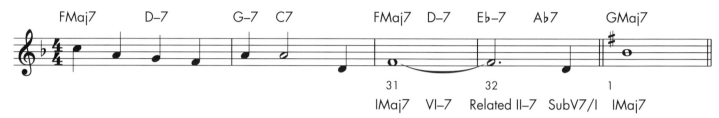

Fig. 8.25. "Days of Wine and Roses," (J. Mercer/H. Mancini), original form with transposed pickup note to fit key of G

In this example, the turnaround leads from F major to A♭ major, aided by a transposed pickup note.

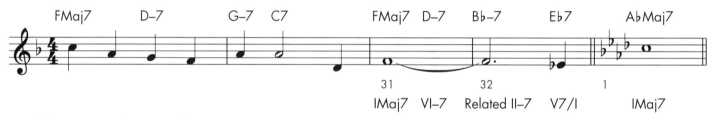

Fig. 8.26. "Days of Wine and Roses," moving to A♭

In this example, the turnaround leads from F major to B major, also with a transposed pickup note.

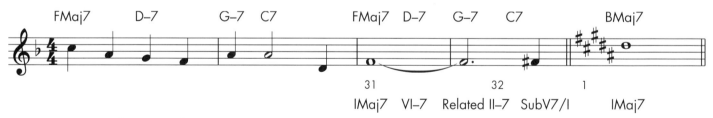

Fig. 8.27. "Days of Wine and Roses," moving to B major

More examples of turnarounds that lead to a new key are shown below.

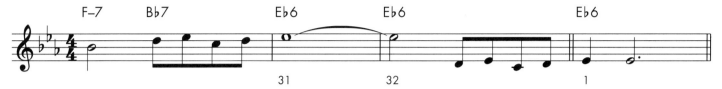

Fig. 8.28. "Isn't It Romantic?" (R. Rodgers/L. Hart), original form

In this example, the turnaround leads from E♭ major to G♭ major. Notice the transposed pickup notes. Here, the long melodic pitch is shortened. As a general rule, you can drop the melody note after it has been established for at least two beats. This new open space in the melody allows you to insert other chord choices that would have clashed with the long E♭ in the lead.

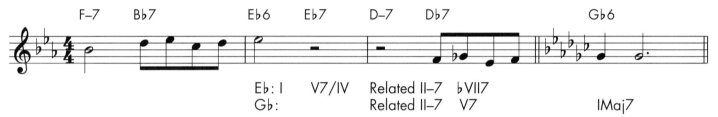

Fig. 8.29. "Isn't It Romantic?" moving to G♭ major

In this example, the turnaround leads from E♭ major to A major. Notice the transposed pickup notes.

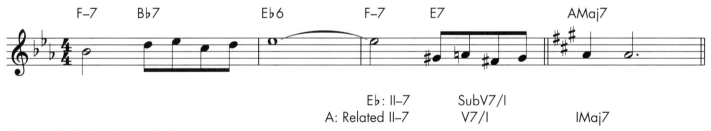

Fig. 8.30. "Isn't It Romantic?" moving to A major

In this example, the turnaround leads from E♭ major to D major. Notice the transposed pickup notes and the reduced rhythmic value of the melodic E♭.

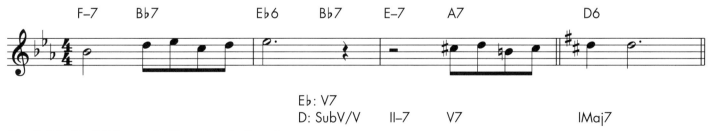

Fig. 8.31. "Isn't It Romantic?" moving to D major

EXERCISES

Practice creating turnarounds that lead to the new keys indicated in the phrase endings below. Work within measures 31 and 32 in each case.

EXERCISE 8.4

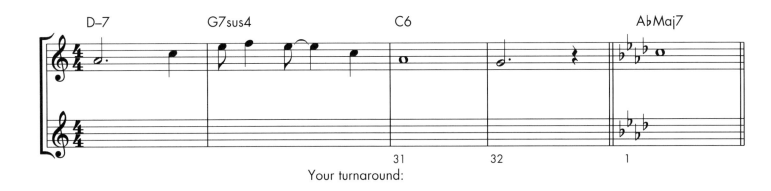

EXERCISE 8.5

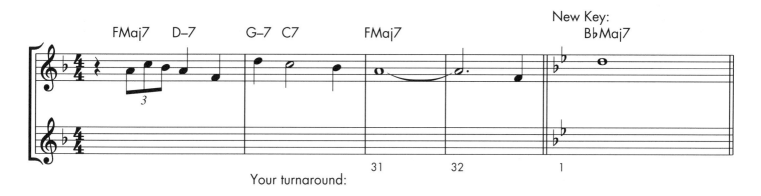

Your turnaround:

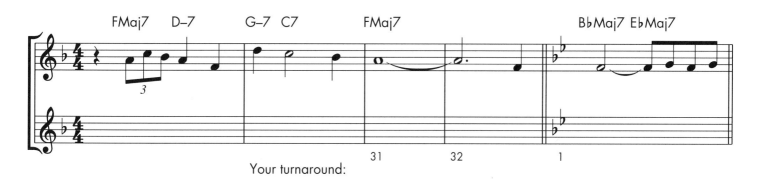

Your turnaround:

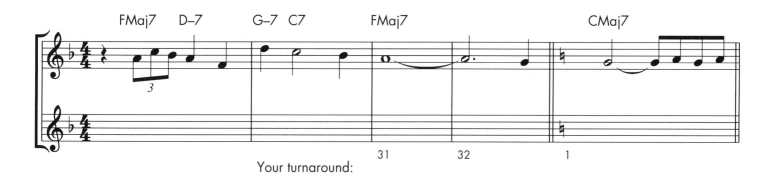

Your turnaround:

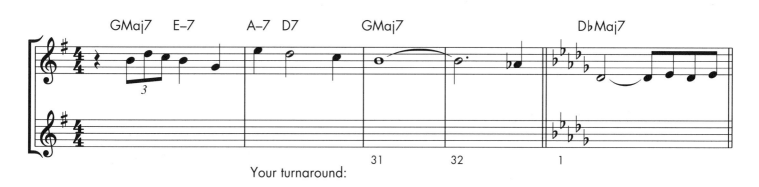

Your turnaround:

EXTENDED ENDINGS AND MODULATORY INTERLUDES

Reharmonization may be used to expand an existing form. Creating an extended ending or modulatory interlude adds dimension to a tune, requiring an alteration of its original harmonic structure.

EXTENDED ENDINGS

Arrangers may opt for an extended ending whenever they want to draw out the last phrase of an arrangement. In some cases, this allows for a long sustained pitch in the melody. It can be used, for example, to demonstrate the beautiful tone, lung capacity, or improvisational imagination of a featured singer or instrumentalist. Think of a long, sustained note sung by a Broadway singer, such as "Evergreen" as sung by Barbra Streisand. Extended endings are also found in rock, as in lead guitar pyrotechnics played over a slowly evolving final progression.

The number of extra chords varies from a minimum of one or two up to eight or more. The meter of the song can influence the length of an extended ending. For example, since each bar of 3/4 time is one beat shorter than 4/4 time, 3/4 tunes can require more extended bars in order to achieve a satisfactory sense of closure.

The following examples illustrate some of the variables.

Fig. 9.1. "Days of Wine and Roses," original form

In the example below, two extra measures were added to the form. The final cadence to IMaj7 is extended by two measures. A deceptive cadence—one that does not resolve in the expected way—is used following the V7 chord, and a series of new chords is inserted into the extended area. The new chords are compatible with the melody and flow toward the final Imaj7 using strong root motion. Melodic material refers to a motive from the song, and the chord changes move with strong root motion toward the final IMaj7 chord.

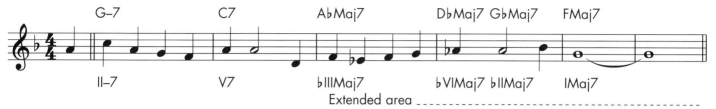

Fig. 9.2. "Days of Wine and Roses," extended ending

Notice that the final IMaj7 in the next example is not in the same key as the rest of the song. Using a final cadential chord in a new key opens up a number of additional cadential choices. Moving to a final I chord in a different key may enhance the sense of surprise created by the extended ending, while at the same time leading the listener to a satisfying conclusion.

The melodic material in the extended ending often consists of a melodic motive from the song. In this case, a melodic extension was written over the new chords. The extended area leads to a final chord in a new key.

Fig. 9.3. "Days of Wine and Roses," with melodic extension and new chords

Fig. 9.4. "Misty," original form

In the example below, the final cadence to IMaj7 is extended by a single measure. A deceptive cadence follows the V7 chord, and two new chords are inserted into the extended area. A compatible melodic extension complements the new chords, and, together, they move forward to the final IMaj7 chord.

Fig. 9.5. "Misty," with extended ending

In fig. 9.6, I use a common deceptive cadential chord (VI–7) at the start of measure 2. I also include a melodic tension and a harmonic tension in the last measure of the example.

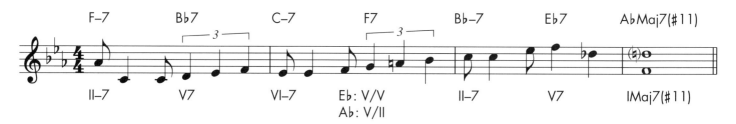

Fig. 9.6. "Misty," extended ending resolving to a new IMaj7

In the next example, notice the use of ♭VIMaj7 as the first chord in the extended ending. Remember that chords based on III and VI can often substitute for I. (See chapter 1.)

After the C♭Maj7 chord creates a deception, the D7 starts a progression with strong root motion to the final IMaj7. The last chord of an extended ending is often a major seventh chord. Major seventh chords suggest a sense of finality even if they are not diatonic to the original key.

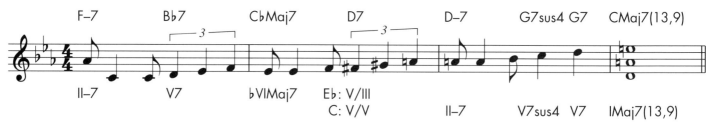

Fig. 9.7. "Misty," extended ending

MODULATORY INTERLUDES

A modulatory interlude is a transition between two choruses of a single song or between two songs in a medley. The modulatory transition includes a change of key. It may vary in duration from as little as two to four measures to eight measures or more.

Fig. 9.8. "Morning of Carnivale (Theme from 'Black Orpheus')" (L. Bonfa), ending, original form

Below, I modulate to a key that is up a minor second from the original. Common modulation distances in pop music often involve a large change of tonality, e.g., up a minor second, up a major second, or up a minor third. From a broad point of view, the arranger may move to any key, but in practical terms, the choice of which new key to move to may be determined by instrumental or vocal range limitations.

A deceptive cadence at the end of the usual song form moves forward into the new key using mostly strong root motion. Think of the first chord of the new key area as a target chord. It is also sometimes helpful to work backwards from the beginning of the new key to the end of the old key.

You may choose to write the new chord progression before the melodic extension, or you may write both at the same time. In either case, the melody uses motivic material from the song, and both chords and melody lead forward into the secondary key. To make the interlude clear to the reader, mark off the beginning and end of the interlude with double bar lines, and establish the new key signature at the start of the next key area.

Fig. 9.9. Secondary key is clearly marked

The reharmonization moves forward with strong root motion, and the melodic material uses a motive from the song. Note the use of VI–7(♭5), a common deceptive cadence chord, in bar 3.

Fig. 9.10. "Days of Wine and Roses," original form

Note again that the reharmonized progression moves forward with strong root motion, and the melodic material uses a motive from the song. Also, the chosen cadential chords are selected to work with the pickup notes leading to the new key. Another common deceptive cadence chord, the ♭IIIMaj7, helps create the modulation.

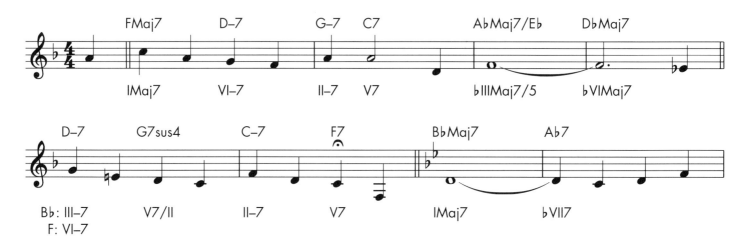

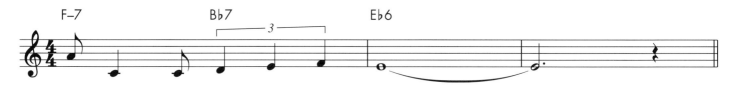

Fig. 9.11. "Days of Wine and Roses," with modulatory interlude

Fig. 9.12. "Misty," original form

In the reharmonization below, note that a VI–7 is used to create a deceptive cadence to the new key.

End of the tune in original key of Eb major:

Start of the tune in Ab major:

Fig. 9.13. "Misty," with modulatory interlude

EXERCISES

In exercises 1–4, create two different extended endings for each phrase. Include Roman numeral analysis of your progressions. Note that you should place a deceptive cadential chord at the start of bar 31. This deceptive chord replaces F6. Be sure not to sustain F6 for two bars before starting your new progression.

EXERCISE 9.1

Original form:

Your extended ending 1:

Your extended ending 2:

EXERCISE 9.2

Original form:

Your extended ending 1:

Your extended ending 2:

EXERCISE 9.3

Original form:

Your extended ending 1:

Your extended ending 2:

EXERCISE 9.4

Original form:

Your extended ending 1:

Your extended ending 2:

Create modulatory interludes for the following examples. The exact length of the interlude is up to you. Include Roman numeral analysis of your progressions.

EXERCISE 9.5

Your extended ending:

EXERCISE 9.6

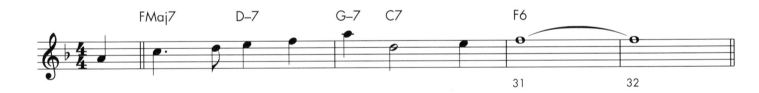

Your extended ending:

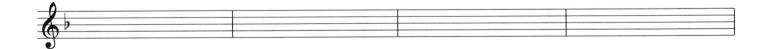

Basic Piano Voicing Techniques

Understanding the basics of piano voicings and the use of common tensions is a first step in creating effective orchestrations of reharmonized melodies.

Chord Tones

To create effective voicings for various chord qualities, be sure to follow these guidelines:

1. Include the root of the chord in the voicing (assuming solo piano with no bass player).

2. Include the basic chord sound.

Chord Type	Basic Chord Sound (Chord Tones)
Triads	3, 5
Sixth chords	3, 6
Seventh chords	3, 7
Dominant 7sus4	4, 7
Minor 7(♭5)	♭3, ♭5, ♭7
Augmented seventh	3, ♯5, ♭7
Diminished seventh	♭3, ♭5, °7

For seventh chords, the basic chord sound consists of chord tones 1, 3, and 7. For sixth chords, the basic chord sound consists of chord tones 1, 3, and 6. The third determines whether the chord is of major or minor quality and the seventh (or sixth) determines the chord function. The flat seventh gives the chord a dominant function, while a major seventh yields a tonic or subdominant function. Chord tone 5 is not considered part of the basic chord sound unless it has been raised or lowered (altered), or is part of a triad. Altered fifths are always considered part of the basic chord sound.

For best results, the basic chord sound (3 and 7) should be placed, or **voiced**, within the following range:

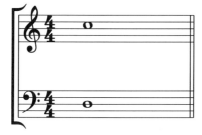

Fig. 10.1. Recommended range for voicing chord tones 3 and 7

The following voicings illustrate the correct placement of basic chord sound for common chord types:

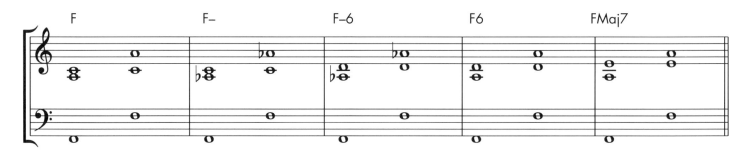

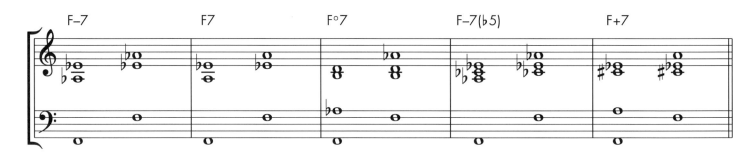

Fig. 10.2. Recommended chord voicings for various chord types

VOICE LEADING

Following voice leading principles will improve the sound of a progression. Voice leading connects notes smoothly from chord to chord with a blended, textural sound. It also makes the voicings easier to play on a keyboard.

Traditional voice leading focuses on the resolution of tendency tones and avoidance of such intervals as parallel fifths, octaves, and certain doublings of pitches within chords. Following voice leading rules will lend a recognizable stylistic sound and chord texture.

Current jazz and pop composers are less concerned with traditional voice leading rules, but still strive for balanced note spacing and reasonably smooth connection from one chord to the next. The following guidelines will help you create voice leading that is consistent with jazz/pop voicing practices.

1. Determine the basic chord sound for each chord.

2. If the root motion moves by perfect fourth or perfect fifth, resolve chord tone 3 in the first chord to chord tone 7 of the second, and chord tone 7 in the first chord to 3 in the second, as shown in the following examples. These resolutions produce a clear harmonic texture and minimize finger movement from chord to chord.

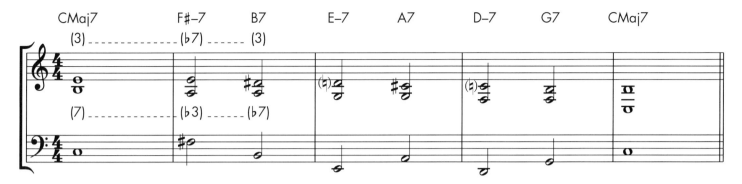

Fig. 10.3. Correct resolutions for chord tones 3 and 7

3. If root motion moves by unison or second, move the voices in parallel motion. Parallel motion means that all voices move up or down by a similar amount. In the example below, D–7 to E–7 finds all voices moving up in diatonic seconds. (Roll over Beethoven!)

Optional: Change the octave position of the root while other parts move in parallel motion. For example, see the movement of E–7 to FMaj7 between measures 2 and 3 below.

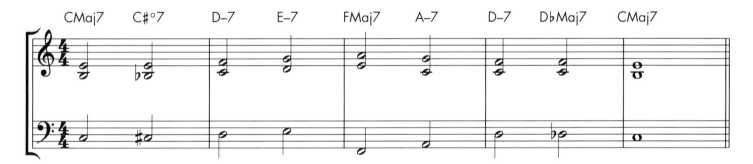

Fig. 10.4. Correct resolutions when voices move in diatonic seconds

4. If roots move by third or sixth, use either parallel or contrary motion between the roots and the upper voices. Contrary motion means that voices move in opposite directions: the bass note moves down, while all other voices move up.

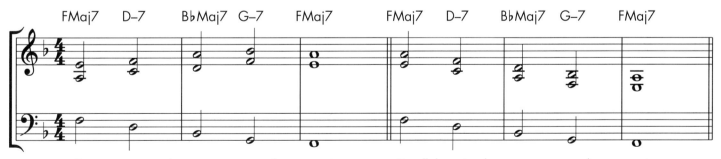

Contrary motion between roots and upper voices   Parallel motion between roots and upper voices

Fig. 10.5. Correct resolutions when roots move by third or sixth

5. If the basic chord sound appears to be heading out of range as the progression is voice-led, change the inversion of chord tones **within** the duration of a single chord and then continue voice leading normally into the next chord. Note that the roots of the chords are not included in the inversion shifts.

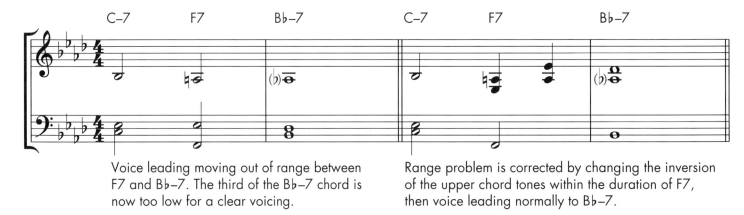

Voice leading moving out of range between F7 and Bb–7. The third of the Bb–7 chord is now too low for a clear voicing.

Range problem is corrected by changing the inversion of the upper chord tones within the duration of F7, then voice leading normally to Bb–7.

Fig. 10.6. Inversions help keep a progression within range

Voice Leading With Tensions

It is common for jazz-style piano voicings to contain additional tensions along with the basic chord tones. The following example shows available tensions placed above the basic chord sound.

G♯ on F♯–7(9) and G♯ on B7(13) are available as tensions on these individual chords, though they are not diatonic to the key, C major. Be sure to include nondiatonic tensions in the chord symbol. Labeling for available tensions that are diatonic to the key is not necessary. In the following examples only nondiatonic tensions are indicated in the chord symbols, even though diatonic tensions are also being used.

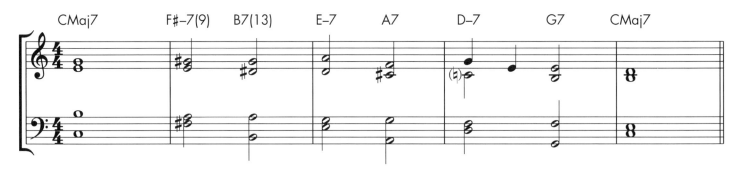

Fig. 10.7. Nondiatonic tensions added to chord voicing symbols above the top note of the three-part voicing

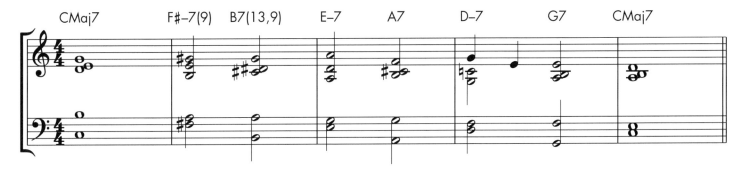

Fig. 10.8. Tensions added between notes of the basic chord sound

The last example shows an additional tension placed a whole or a half step below the basic chord sound. **It is generally good practice to keep all tensions above the F found on the fourth line of the bass clef in order to avoid a muddy sound.**

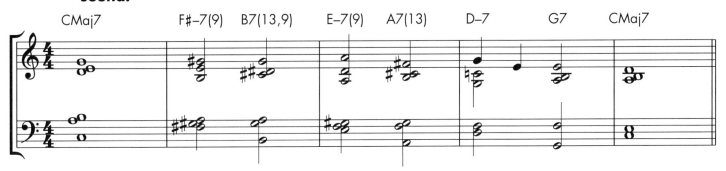

Fig. 10.9. Tensions added below basic chord sound in second and third measures

VOICE LEADING OF INVERSIONS

Inverted chord structures should include all chord tones and use no more than one octave between adjacent voices. The only exception is the distance between the lowest two voices. If you are striving for a traditional texture, do not double the bass note when it is the third or the seventh of the chord. In the following examples, the "x" indicates chord voicings that would be inappropriate in a traditional context. The checkmark indicates chord voicings that would work well.

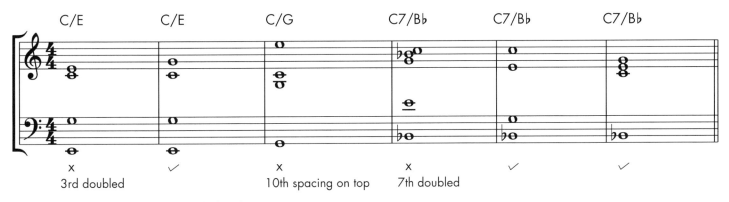

Fig. 10.10. Voicings of inverted chords

Tensions are less commonly voiced when a chord is inverted, since the combination of additional notes in the voicing and the lack of a root in the bottom voice make the harmonic meaning of the chord difficult to understand. When tensions are used with inverted chords, they are most often found in the lead voice. Keep all tensions above fourth-line F in the bass clef.

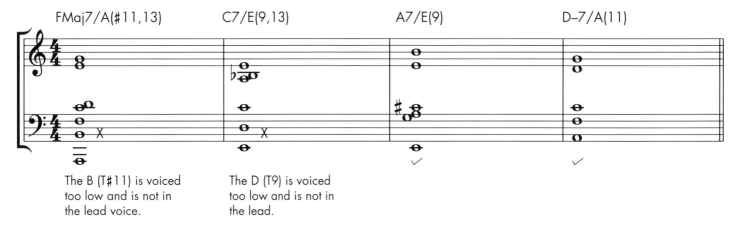

The B (T♯11) is voiced too low and is not in the lead voice.

The D (T9) is voiced too low and is not in the lead.

Fig. 10.11. Some common errors

Non-chord tones (tensions 9, 11, 13) found in the lowest voice produce a hybrid voicing. (See chapter 14.)

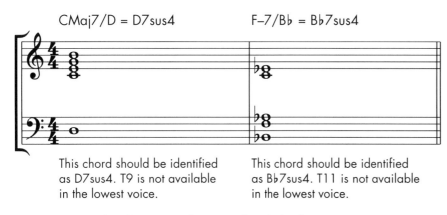

This chord should be identified as D7sus4. T9 is not available in the lowest voice.

This chord should be identified as B♭7sus4. T11 is not available in the lowest voice.

Fig. 10.12. Chords incorrectly notated as hybrid voicings

It is usually best to move away from an inverted chord by step. Inversions function as passing chords; they rarely begin or conclude harmonic phrases. The use of an inversion does not change the functional analysis of a progression in any way. Roman numerals can be written as usual with the addition of the inversion.

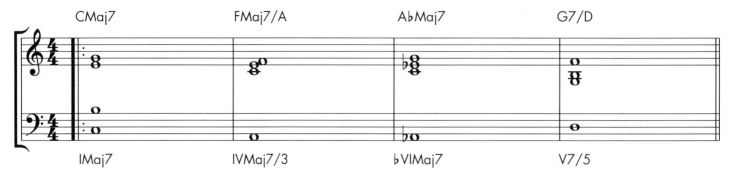

Fig. 10.13. Inversion functions as a passing chord

Special problems occur when using the third inversion of a seventh chord. "Third inversion" means that the chord is voiced with the seventh in the bass. In a majority of cases, the chord will sound ambiguous if it is not preceded by a root-position voicing of the same chord. The examples below sound like hybrid voicings, not major seventh chords with the seventh in the bass. (See chapter 14.)

Play fig. 10.14. If the chord (E, G, and C, over B) is played as the first chord in a phrase, it will be heard as a B chord structure with tensions ♭9, 11, and ♭13. The second chord (F, A, C, over E) will be heard as an E chord structure with ♭9, 11, and ♭13. The bass note strongly influences how a chord is heard, unless the chord is clearly placed inside a diatonic progression. (G7/F moving to Cmaj7 is an exception to this rule. In very simple harmonic contexts such as V7 to I, the basic cadence will be heard despite the use of third inversion.)

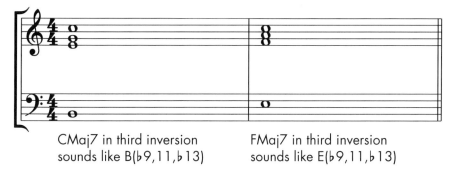

CMaj7 in third inversion
sounds like B(♭9,11,♭13)

FMaj7 in third inversion
sounds like E(♭9,11,♭13)

Fig. 10.14. Inversions may be misheard in context

One way to resolve ambiguity is to place root-position voicings in strong rhythmic positions. When a root-position voicing is used as the first chord of a phrase, it establishes the diatonic context for the following two chords.

Without a diatonic context, the chords in third inversion will likely sound like hybrid chords derived from the altered dominant scale. They will not blend smoothly into most diatonic progressions.

For a smooth, traditional sound, precede each third inversion chord with the same chord in root position.

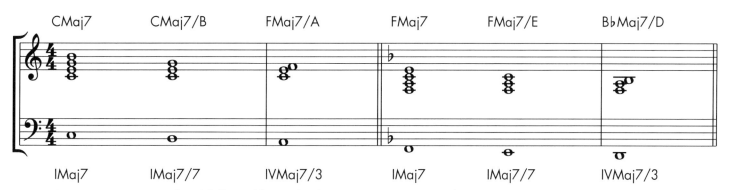

Fig. 10.15. Root position chord followed by its third inversion

EXERCISES

EXERCISE 10.1

Voice lead the following progression using chord tones only.

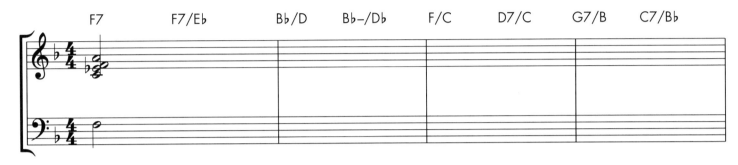

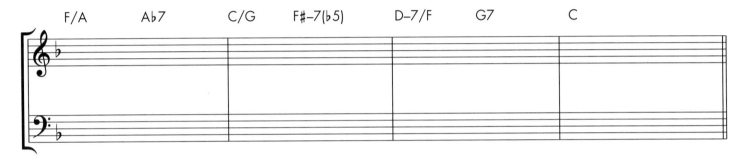

EXERCISE 10.2

Voice lead the following progression using chord tones and tensions. Use three to six notes in each voicing.

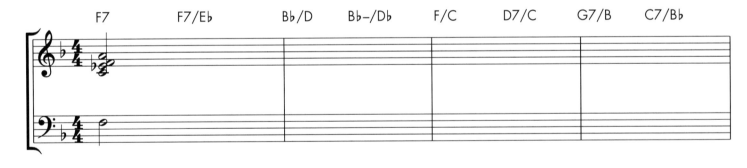

EXERCISE 10.3

Voice lead the following progression, using the minimum number of notes needed to capture the basic chord sound.

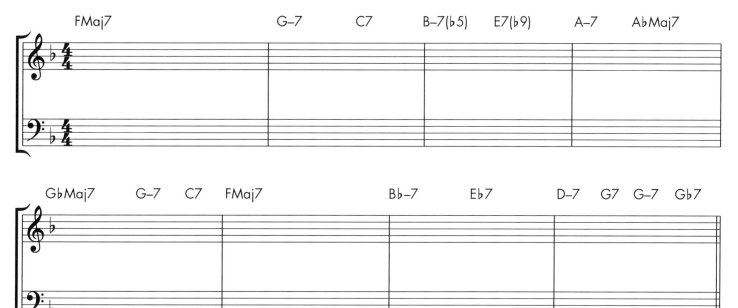

FMaj7   G–7   C7   B–7(♭5)   E7(♭9)   A–7   A♭Maj7

G♭Maj7   G–7   C7   FMaj7   B♭–7   E♭7   D–7   G7   G–7   G♭7

EXERCISE 10.4

Repeat the same voicings, using one available tension **above** the basic chord sound.

FMaj7   G–7   C7   B–7(♭5)   E7(♭9)   A–7   A♭Maj7

G♭Maj7   G–7   C7   FMaj7   B♭–7   E♭7   D–7   G7   G–7   G♭7

EXERCISE 10.5

Repeat the same voicings, using one available tension **above** the basic chord sound
and another **between** the notes that form the basic chord sound.

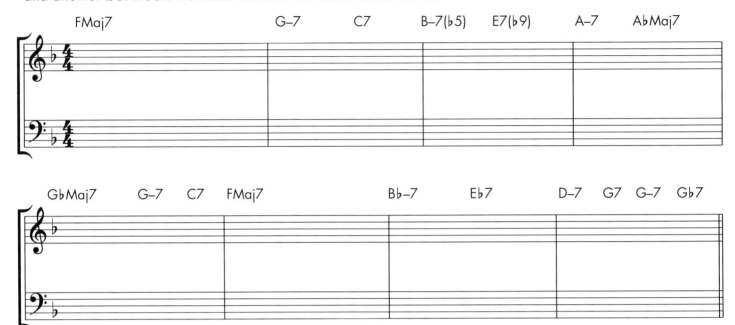

EXERCISE 10.6

Repeat the same voicings, using available tensions **above, between,** and a **step below** the basic
chord sound.

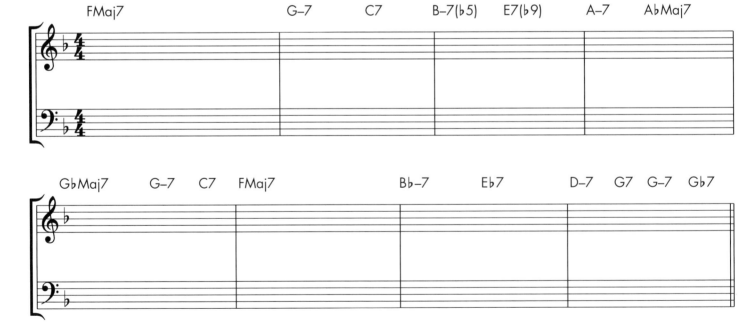

LINE CLICHÉS

A line cliché is a stepwise descending or ascending line that moves against a single stationary chord. Line clichés may be used to reharmonize melodic phrases that are largely diatonic to a single key. Famous line cliché tunes include "My Funny Valentine," "Michelle," and the "Bond" theme from the early James Bond films.

Fig. 11.1. Typical descending line cliché

Fig. 11.2. Typical ascending line cliché

In order to use a line cliché as a reharmonization technique, find a melodic phrase in which most of the notes are diatonic to the key. Then, eliminate the original progression and insert a single major or minor chord that is compatible with the melody notes. You can then embellish this chord with a line cliché. The example below illustrates this process.

Fig. 11.3. Original form

Fig. 11.4. Phrase reharmonized with a single chord that is harmonically compatible with the melodic material

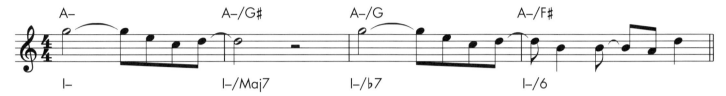

Fig. 11.5. Line cliché added: chromatic line descends in half steps against a static minor chord

The next example shows a chromatic line that rises and falls against the static minor chord. The line cliché movement is most often in half steps between the fifth and root of the chord being embellished.

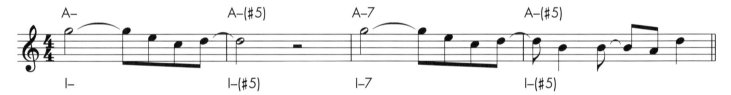

Fig. 11.6. Line cliché

Although most line clichés move in half-step increments, whole step motion between the fifth and the root is also possible. Fig. 11.7 illustrates a line cliché derived from the Aeolian scale.

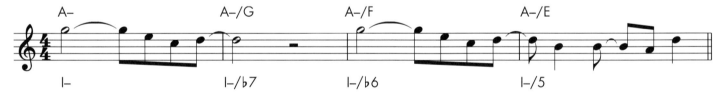

Fig. 11.7. Aeolian line cliché

The harmonic rhythm of the line cliché also may be varied. The example below doubles the number of chords per measure.

Fig. 11.8. Line cliché with faster harmonic rhythm

The example in fig. 11.9 is a good candidate for a line cliché. All the melody notes are diatonic to a single key.

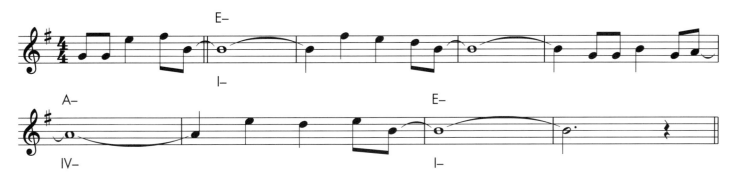

Fig. 11.9. Original form

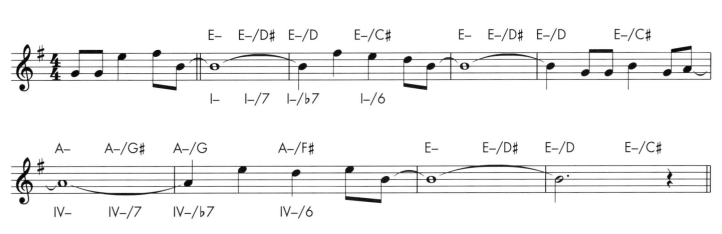

Fig 11.10. Line cliché added

The next example is also reharmonized with line clichés. The moving line illustrates that the descending (or ascending) line does not have to move exclusively by half steps. Whole-step motion also works, and is sometimes needed to prevent melody/harmony clashes.

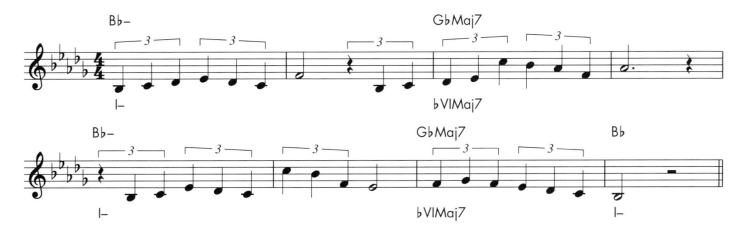

Fig. 11.11. Original form

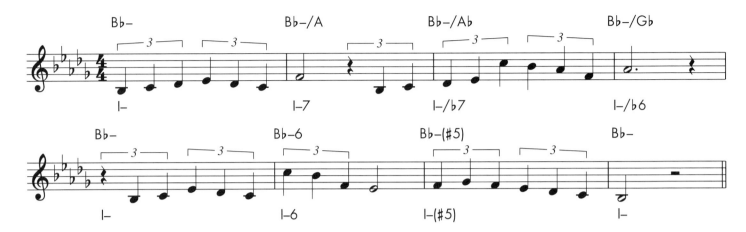

Fig. 11.12. Line cliché added

The harmonic rhythm should fit with the performance tempo. If the song is played at a fast tempo, a harmonic rhythm of one chord per measure will sound smooth.

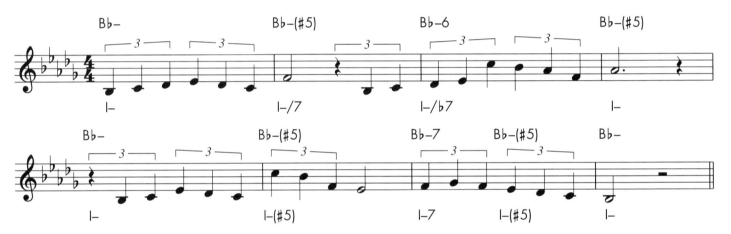

Fig. 11.13. A faster tempo calls for a slower harmonic rhythm.

If performance tempo is very fast, an even more sparse and extended harmonic rhythm would be a good choice.

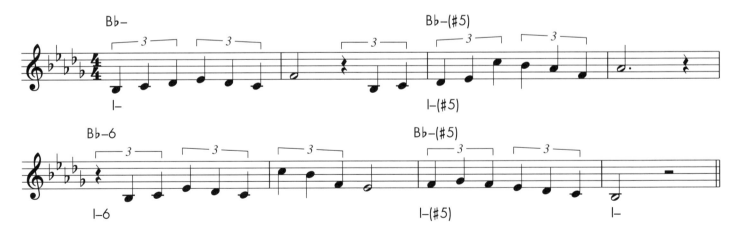

Fig. 11.14. A very fast tempo calls for an even slower harmonic rhythm.

Line clichés may also be used to reharmonize melodies in major keys.

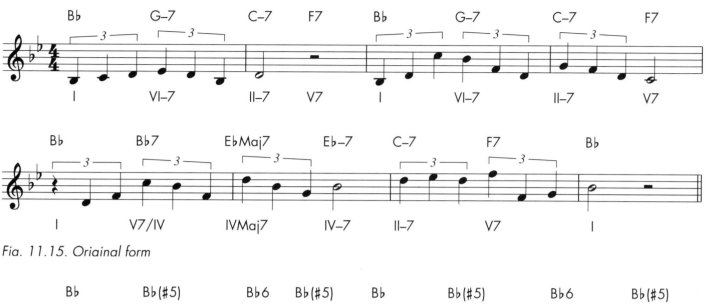

Fig. 11.15. Original form

Fig. 11.16. Reharmonized using line clichés

Although line clichés are found on the I chord more often than on other diatonic chords, a short line cliché (one measure or less) may be applied to any diatonic chord.

The line cliché allows the writer to sustain a particular chord while adding momentum to the progression. However, repeated use of a line cliché on a chord other than the "I" may cause the listener to hear the chord being embellished by the line cliché as a new I chord. Overuse of this technique may weaken the sense of key within the progression.

The example below uses short line clichés based on II–7 and IVMaj7. Notice the increased sense of motion and the varied rhythmic placement of the lines. Each line cliché leads to its target chord by stepwise motion.

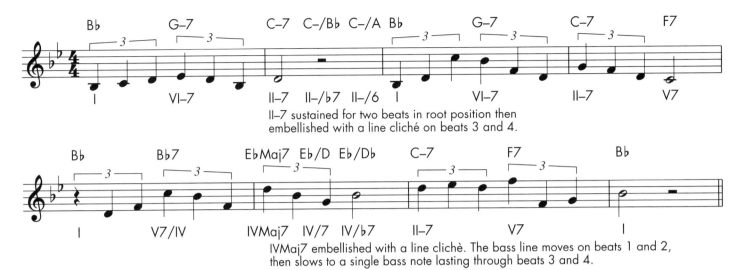

II–7 sustained for two beats in root position then
embellished with a line cliché on beats 3 and 4.

IVMaj7 embellished with a line cliché. The bass line moves on beats 1 and 2,
then slows to a single bass note lasting through beats 3 and 4.

Fig. 11.17. Line cliché based on II–7 and IVMaj7

Here is a different example.

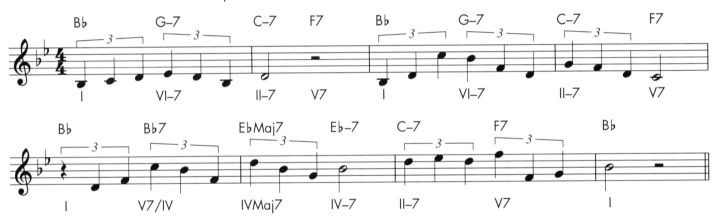

Fig. 11.18. Original form

Short passing notes against a single chord may be used in the same spirit as a full line
cliché. The reharmonized example below uses stepwise, passing sevenths in the bass to
increase the sense of movement within the chord progression.

The example below is reharmonized with passing sevenths in the bass. Notice that a
chord in root position always precedes a chord voiced over its seventh.

Fig. 11.19. Line cliché with passing sevenths in the bass

EXERCISES

Reharmonize the following examples using line clichés. Analyze your result using Roman numerals.

EXERCISE 11.1

"An August Moon" (R. Felts), original form

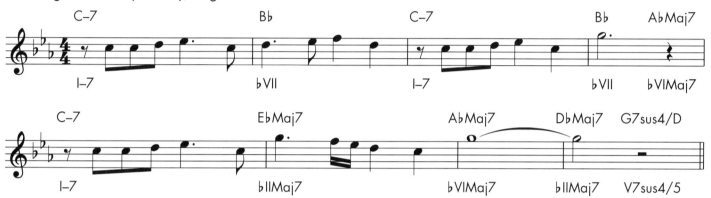

Your reharmonization 1:

Your reharmonization 2:

EXERCISE 11.2

"Homecoming" (R. Felts), original form

Your reharmonization 1:

Your reharmonization 2:

12

DIMINISHED SEVENTH CHORDS

Diminished seventh chords are common in standard tunes of the early- to mid-twentieth century. Contemporary composers and arrangers have shown less affection for diminished chords and often reharmonize many of the original diminished sevenths when developing new arrangements of older standards.

Using or not using diminished sevenths in musical progressions is a personal artistic choice. It is not necessary or desirable to reharmonize every diminished seventh chord found in standard tunes.

Every diminished seventh chord contains two tritones. Tritones are the active ingredients within dominant seventh chords. They create instability in the sound of the chord and demand resolution. This instability is due in part to the melodic voice-leading tendencies of each note in a diminished chord.

In the example below, the C#°7 contains a C# pitch with a tendency to resolve up to D, and a B♭ pitch with a melodic tendency to resolve to A. In addition, the C# and G form a tritone interval. The dominant or tritone energy and sound is very familiar. We expect it to resolve into a more stable, restful target chord.

Every diminished seventh chord contains two tritones:

Fig. 12.1. Diminished chord with tritones

The following progression illustrates a classic diminished pattern, in which the tritones of C#°7 resolve into D–7. In this example, C#°7 has the same functional sound as A7(♭9): V7 of II. The chord C#°7 functions as A7(♭9) without the root.

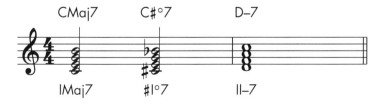

Fig. 12.2. A typical diminished chord resolution

Four dominant seventh chords are related to a given diminished seventh chord. These four dominant chords (with or without their related II–7s) are the most common choices for reharmonizing a diminished seventh. Each of these dominant chords contains one of the tritones found in the original diminished seventh.

To find the four dominant chords related to a given diminished seventh chord, look down a major third below each chord tone in the diminished seventh.

Fig. 12.3. Chord tones of C♯°7

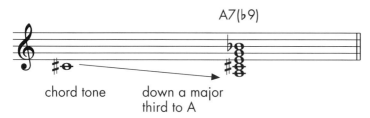

Fig. 12.4. A major third below the chord tone C♯ is A. C♯°7 can be reharmonized with A7 or A7(♭9).

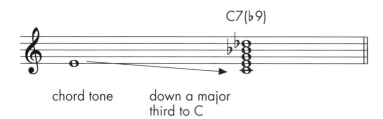

Fig. 12.5. A major third below the chord tone E is C. C♯°7 can be reharmonized with C7 or C7(♭9).

Fig. 12.6. A major third below the chord tone G is E♭. C♯°7 can be reharmonized with E♭7 or E♭7(♭9).

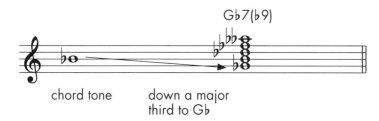

Fig. 12.7. A major third below the chord tone B♭ is G♭. C♯°7 can be reharmonized with G♭7 or G♭7(♭9).

Another way to find the chords related to a diminished seventh is to locate the note a minor second below each chord tone of the diminished chord.

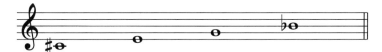

Fig. 12.8. Chord tones of C#°7

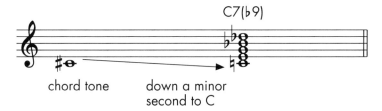

Fig. 12.9. A minor second below the chord tone C# is C. C#°7 can be reharmonized with C7 or C7(b9).

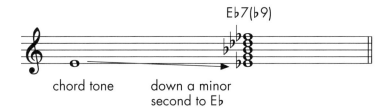

Fig. 12.10. A minor second below the chord tone E is Eb. C#°7 can be reharmonized with Eb7 or Eb7(b9).

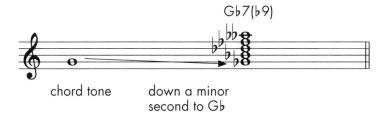

Fig. 12.11. A minor second below the chord tone G is Gb. C#°7 can be reharmonized with Gb7 or Gb7(b9).

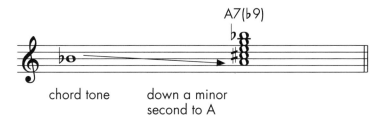

Fig. 12.12. A minor second below the chord tone Bb is A. C#°7 can be reharmonized with A7 or A7(b9).

In practice, the substitute chord is determined by the melody/harmony relationship and by the root motion into the target chord.

Diminished seventh chords that move up by half step to a chord in root position are most often reharmonized with dominant sevenths that are a perfect fifth above or a minor second above the target.

Of the possible choices in the example below, A7 (V7 of the D–7) and E♭7 (substitute V7 of the D–7) form the strongest resolutions to the root of the target chord.

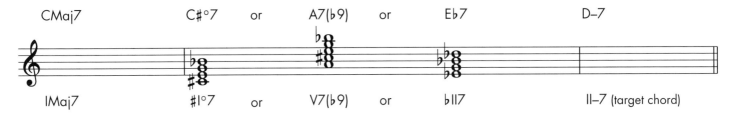

Fig. 12.13. C#°7 has the same function as A7(♭9) or E♭7. A7(♭9) and E♭7 are the standard reharmonization choices for this example.

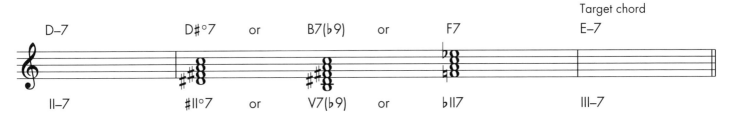

Fig. 12.14. D#°7 has the same function as B7(♭9) or F7. B7(♭9) and F7 are the standard reharmonization choices for this example.

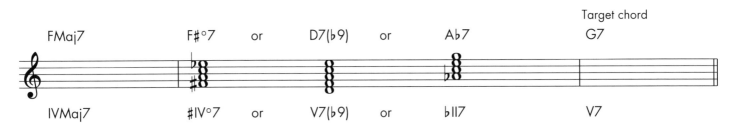

Fig. 12.15. F#°7 has the same function as D7(♭9) or A♭7. D7(♭9) and A♭7 are the standard reharmonization choices for this example.

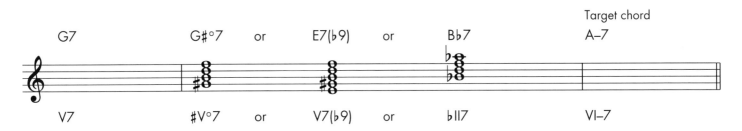

Fig. 12.16. G#°7 has the same function as E7(♭9) or B♭7. E7(♭9) and B♭7 are the standard reharmonization choices for this example.

The following example shows another common diminished seventh pattern. The descending root motion changes the choice of reharmonization. Replacing the diminished seventh chord with the dominant or substitute dominant (subV) of the target chord does not fit as smoothly as in the ascending patterns.

Fig. 12.17. A common diminished seventh pattern

Fig. 12.18. Tritones in the Eb°7 chord

Reharmonizing with the seventh chord built off of the minor second below each chord tone yields and Cb7, F7, D7, and Ab7.

Fig. 12.19. Target chord D–7 being approached by each of the four dominant seventh substitutions

None of the four choices has an obvious dominant cadence leading into the D–7 target chord. That is, none of the dominant sevenths related to Eb°7 is V7 of D–7 or subV7 of D–7. Under these conditions, look for the chord that is most strongly related to the **chord structure** of the original diminished seventh chord.

Since Cb7 contains nearly all of the chord tones of Eb°7, it becomes the leading candidate to replace Eb°7. This reasoning is supported by traditional classical music theory, in which diminished sevenths are considered incomplete forms of dominant seventh chords. According to this system, Eb°7 serves as a Cb7 chord with the root missing.

Fig. 12.20. "You Took Advantage of Me" (R. Rodgers/L. Hart), original form

Below, both original diminished seventh chords are reharmonized. The A7(♭9) contains the same tritone as C♯°7 and pulls strongly toward the D–7 target chord. The B7(♭9) contains the same tritone as E♭°7. Although it does not pull strongly toward its D–7 target chord, the B7(♭9) works in context because it sounds similar to E♭°7. It also forms an acceptable melody/harmony relationship.

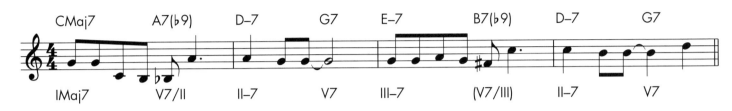

Fig. 12.21. Diminished seventh chords replaced/reharmonized with dominant seventh chords

Fig. 12.22. Common tones found between E♭7 and B7(♭9)

Fig. 12.23. Diminished seventh chords replaced/reharmonized with dominant seventh chords

Here, the original C♯°7 in measure 1 is reharmonized with E♭7. E♭7 contains the same tritone as C♯°7 and functions as a substitute dominant seventh leading to D–7.

Fig. 12.24. Notice the common tones found in both C♯°7 and E♭7.

To summarize:

1. When reharmonizing diminished seventh chords, choose a dominant chord that shares one of the tritone intervals found in the original diminished seventh.

2. When possible, also choose a chord that forms a dominant cadence into the target chord.

3. When a dominant cadence to the target chord is not available, choose a dominant chord that shares a considerable number of chord tones with the original diminished seventh. Be sure it is compatible with the melody.

DOMINANT CHORDS AND THEIR RELATED II–7 CHORDS

In fig. 12.25, dominant seventh chords used as reharmonizations are accompanied by their related II–7 chords. The total number of chords per measure (the harmonic rhythm) has increased. Using the related II–7 chords may cause the progression to seem too busy. This is especially true in up-tempo arrangements.

Fig. 12.25. "You Took Advantage of Me," diminished seventh chords replaced/reharmonized with dominant seventh chords and their related II–7 chords

A further variation uses chromatic II–V7 patterns created by inserting tritone substitutions for A7(♭9) and B7(♭9). (A chromatic II–V7 pattern is made up of a minor seventh chord or a minor 7(♭5) followed by a dominant seventh a half step below. The root motion between the two chords is chromatic and the two chords sound subdominant to dominant in the same spirit as regular II–V7 patterns.)

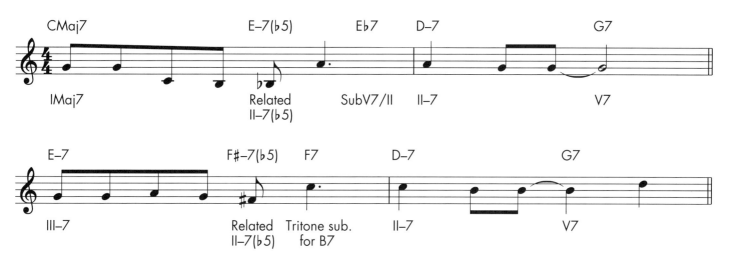

Fig. 12.26. "You Took Advantage of Me," diminished seventh chords replaced and reharmonized with dominant seventh chords and their related II–7 chords

EXERCISES

Reharmonize the diminished chords in the following examples. Include a complete Roman numeral analysis of the original form and of your reharmonizations.

EXERCISE 12.1

Original form:

Your reharmonization:

EXERCISE 12.2

Original form:

Your reharmonization:

EXERCISE 12.3

Original form:

Your reharmonization:

EXERCISE 12.4

Original form:

Your reharmonization:

EXERCISE 12.5

Original form:

Your reharmonization:

EXERCISE 12.6

Original form:

Your reharmonization:

EXERCISE 12.7

Original form:

Your reharmonization:

MODAL REHARMONIZATION

A mode is a scale. In practical use, the terms "mode" and "scale" are interchangeable. Ionian mode (the major scale) and Aeolian mode (the natural minor scale) are the two most widely used modes. They contain patterns of whole and half steps on which the remaining modes are based.

Taking the major scale as a starting point, you may think of Dorian mode as the pattern of whole and half steps that results by starting and stopping on the second step of the major mode. The Phrygian mode is the pattern you get if you start and stop on the third scale step. Lydian mode starts on the fourth step, Mixolydian mode on the fifth step, and Aeolian on the sixth step. Each of these combinations of whole and half steps produces a scale or mode that has a specific color or mood.

Chords that are diatonic to each mode are built by stacking diatonic thirds above each pitch in the modal scale.

Each mode contains a **characteristic note** that represents the heart of its unique sound. The diatonic chords that contain the mode's characteristic note are called **characteristic chords**. A **modal cadence** is created when a characteristic chord is used to approach a I chord in a particular mode. The chord qualities and the root motions associated with these characteristic chords are specialized, and are different from modal patterns found in the Ionian (major) mode. The unique sound of these modal cadences may be used to reharmonize melodic phrases.

We will consider characteristic cadential patterns from three minor modes (Dorian, Phyrgian, and Aeolian) and from two major modes (Lydian and Mixolydian).

DORIAN MODE: The I tonic chord in Dorian mode is minor (I– or I–7). The Dorian mode is the scale starting on the second degree of a major scale. The characteristic note of Dorian mode is 6 (A-natural in C Dorian).

characteristic
note

Fig. 13.1. Dorian scale in C

Each of the cadential chords shown below contains the characteristic note. Moving to I–7 with the following chord combinations will create cadences with a distinctive Dorian color.

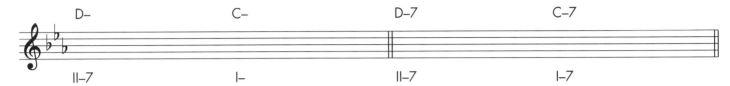

Fig. 13.2. Dorian cadence from D–7 to C minor

Hint: If the theoretical explanation of modal cadences leaves you feeling confused, skip the theory (at least, at first), and notice whether the cadential chords are major or minor. Then, memorize the Roman numeral combinations shown in each modal key.

In modal reharmonization, you may use both triads and seventh chords. For study purposes, consider each resolution to C minor as a separate cadence. Any or all of the combinations leading to a I– triad or I–7 will produce a Dorian color. Variations of the cadential chords (triad and sevenths) may be used freely.

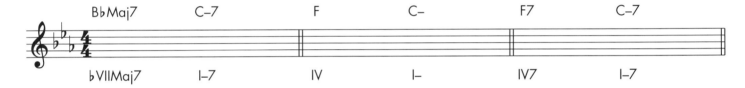

Fig. 13.3. Dorian chord cadence to C minor

One- or two-chord cadences derived from the same modal scale may also be used to approach I–7, the tonic chord of Dorian.

Fig. 13.4. Two-chord Dorian cadences to C minor

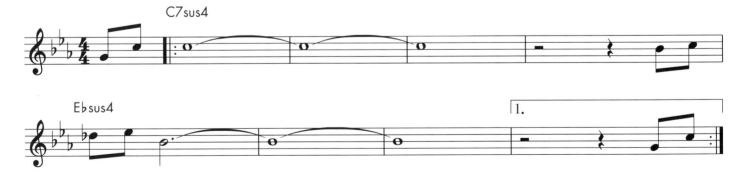

Fig. 13.5. "Maiden Voyage" (H. Hancock), original form

In the reharmonization, C7sus4 is replaced with C–7. Dorian is a minor mode. To create a Dorian color, a I– or I–7 must be used. As always, the I chord is placed in a strong rhythmic position to maintain a clear sense of tonality. The I–7 is then approached by a two-chord cadence derived from Dorian mode.

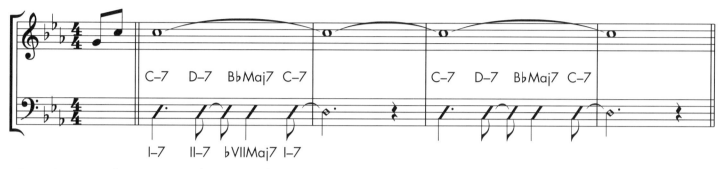

Fig. 13.6. "Maiden Voyage" reharmonized with a Dorian cadence

Here, the tune is reharmonized with Dorian modal cadences and supported by a sustained pitch on scale degree 1 of its key—known as a **tonic pedal tone.**

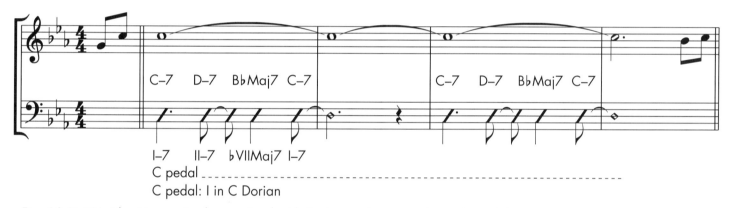

Fig. 13.7. "Maiden Voyage" reharmonized with Dorian cadences and a tonic pedal tone

A tune like "Maiden Voyage," with its long sustained melodic lines, is ideal for modal reharmonization. The example below shows the Dorian cadences transposed to G minor (Dorian) over a G pedal. The melody remains unchanged.

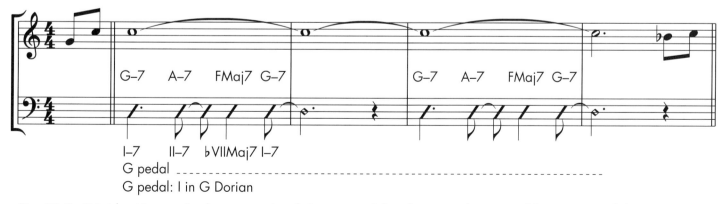

Fig. 13.8. "Maiden Voyage," reharmonized with Dorian modal cadences and supported by a tonic pedal

The supporting modal cadences are transposed to B♭ minor (Dorian) while the melody remains unchanged.

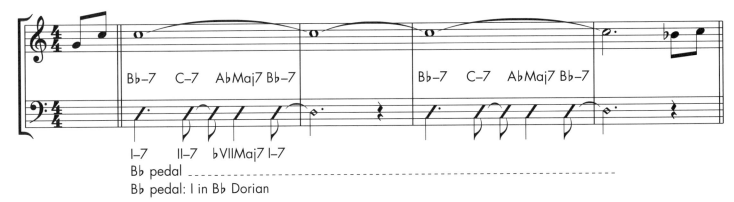

Fig. 13.9. "Maiden Voyage," reharmonized in a different modal key

The next melodic fragment, from "The Duke," is entirely diatonic to the D Dorian scale. This makes it a prime candidate for reharmonization with a Dorian cadence. Not all parts of the melody can accommodate Dorian reharmonization, however. As with many tunes, some segments of the melody fit different modal cadences, while others contain too many chromatic tones to use any modal cadence.

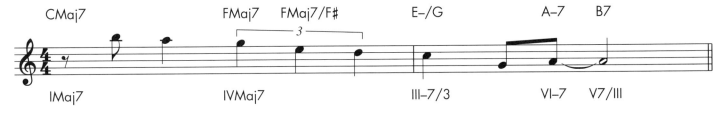

Fig. 13.10. "The Duke" (D. Brubeck), original form

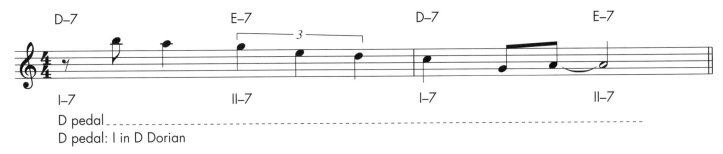

Fig. 13.11. "The Duke," reharmonized with a Dorian cadence and supported by a tonic pedal

PHRYGIAN MODE: The I chord in Phrygian mode is minor and is the tonic of its key. Its characteristic note is ♭2 (D♭ in C Phrygian).

Fig. 13.12. Phrygian scale in C

Each of the cadential chords below contains the characteristic note. Moving to I–7 with these chord combinations will create cadences with a unique Phrygian color.

Notice whether the cadential chords are major or minor. You may use both triads and seventh chords, as indicated in the examples. For study purposes, consider each resolution to C minor as a separate cadence. Any or all of these combinations leading to I– triad or I–7 will produce a Phrygian color. Variations of the cadential chords (triad and sevenths) may be used freely.

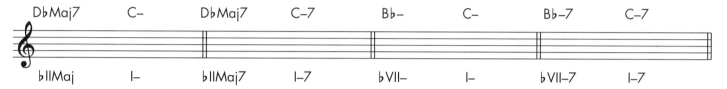

Fig. 13.13. Phrygian cadences to C minor

Fig. 13.14. "Maiden Voyage," original form

Below, the I–7 chord is approached by two Phrygian cadence chords. F–7 (I–7) substitutes for Eb7sus4 because it works well with the melody.

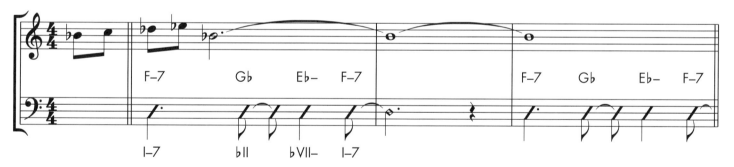

Fig. 13.15. "Maiden Voyage," reharmonized with Phrygian cadences from another key

Dorian and Phrygian modal cadences must resolve to a minor target chord. However, the tonality (key) of the reharmonized phrase is not always the same as the original phrase.

Choose a I–7 chord and modal cadential chords that do not clash with the melody. A single melodic fragment may be supported in several different keys. Examine melody/harmony combinations carefully. Avoid unwanted b9s, tritones, or melody/harmony relationships that are not diatonic to the modal key.

Remember that ♭9 intervals between 1 and ♭2 are part of Phrygian writing and that tritones between 1 and ♯4 are part of Lydian writing. The **accidental** or **unstructured** use of these melody/harmony combinations will create problems in your reharmonizations.

If working within the Dorian mode, both melody and chords should be diatonic to a particular Dorian scale. In a Phrygian example, both melody and chords should be diatonic to a particular Phrygian scale.

With certain melodies, more than one modal tonality (key) will be available.

The following example is the same melody reharmonized using a different Phrygian scale. It is in a different key, changed from F minor (Phrygian) to C minor (Phrygian). This change of key is possible because the melody does not create unwanted ♭9 or tritone melody/harmony combinations. The D♭ melody note against C minor in bar 1 resolves by step and is ♭2, the characteristic note of the Phrygian mode. When the melody/harmony combinations agree, the reharmonization is successful.

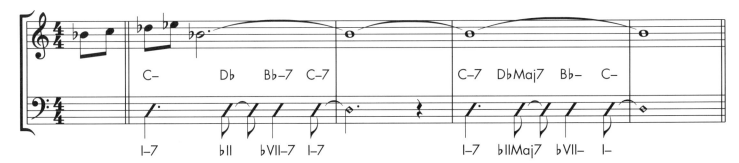

Fig. 13.16. "Maiden Voyage," reharmonized with Phrygian cadences from another key

Changing between modal key centers allows you to reharmonize longer melodic sections. Many melodies will include pitches that only fit certain modal keys. Changing keys allows you to maintain an overall modal texture in your reharmonization, while adjusting the specific modes and keys to fit individual melodic phrases.

Since it often takes several bars for the textural effect of modal writing to become obvious to the listener, remaining in each modal key for at least four bars is a good way to ensure that the modal color is clearly heard. You might also choose to use different modal key areas just for the sake of variety.

Fig. 13.17. "If You Knew" (R. Felts), original form

Fig. 13.18. "If You Knew," reharmonized with Phrygian cadences from another key

AEOLIAN MODE: The I chord in Aeolian mode is minor (I– or I–7) and is the tonic chord of its key. The characteristic note of Aeolian mode is ♭6 (A♭ in key of C minor).

Fig. 13.19. Aeolian scale in C

Each of the cadential chords shown below contain the characteristic note. Moving to I–7 with the following chord combinations will create distinctively Aeolian cadences.

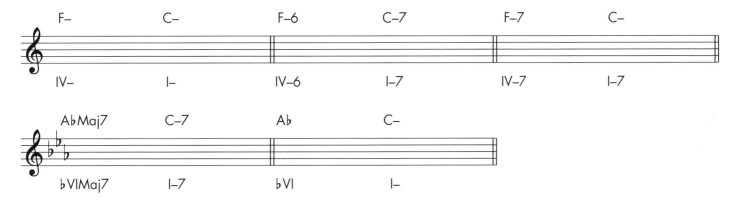

Fig. 13.20. Aeolian cadential chords with characteristic ♭6

Note whether the cadential chords are major or minor, and memorize the Roman numeral combinations shown in each modal key. You may use both triads and seventh chords, as indicated in the examples. For study purposes, consider each resolution to C minor as a separate cadence. Any or all of these combinations leading to a I– triad or I–7 will produce an Aeolian color. Variations of the cadential chords (triad and sevenths) may be used freely.

Fig. 13.21. Aeolian cadences to C minor

Fig. 13.22. "Blue in Green" (M. Davis), original form

Fig. 13.23. "Blue in Green," reharmonized with Aeolian cadences and a new I chord

Fig. 13.24. "Blue in Green," reharmonized with Aeolian cadences and a new I chord

Fig. 13.25 shows Aeolian cadences used as modal interchange chords. The key is C major. The overall phrase does not produce a completely C Aeolian color, but the individual cadential chords are borrowed from the C Aeolian scale. They contribute some Aeolian color without transposing the entire phrase to Aeolian mode. This is an example of modal interchange from the C Aeolian scale.

Fig. 13.25. "Blue in Green," reharmonized with additional Aeolian cadences and a new I chord

Writing true modal phrases requires that diatonic cadential chords resolve to the I chord of that mode. In the example above, the modal cadential chords from C Aeolian (a minor mode) resolve into a Cmaj7 target chord. This combination of minor and major chords based on the same overall pitch center is called modal interchange. (Review modal interchange concepts in chapter 5.)

Fig. 13.26 shows Aeolian cadences used as modal interchange chords. The new key is D major. As in the previous example, the individual cadential chords are borrowed from the D Aeolian scale, adding Aeolian color without transposing the entire phrase to Aeolian mode. This is an example of modal interchange from the D Aeolian scale.

Fig. 13.26. "Blue in Green," reharmonized with Aeolian cadences and a new I chord

LYDIAN MODE: The I chord in Lydian mode is major. The I chord may take the form of a major triad, a major seventh chord, or a major 7(#11) chord. The characteristic note of Lydian mode is #4, also spelled as #11 (F# in C Lydian).

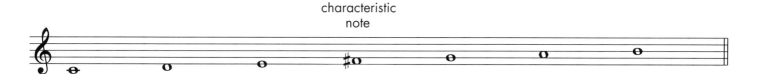

Fig. 13.27. Lydian scale in C

Moving to the I with the following chord combinations will create cadences with a unique Lydian color. Consider each resolution to C as a separate cadence.

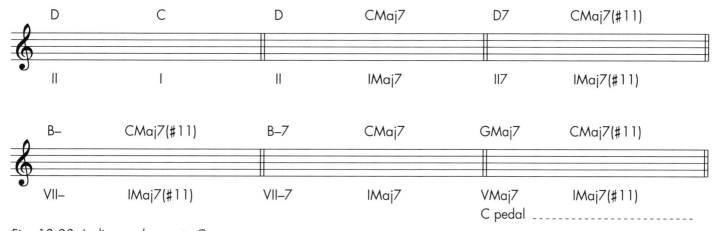

Fig. 13.28. Lydian cadences to C

The tonic pedal tone used with the example above (VMaj7 to IMaj7) helps the cadence maintain its Lydian character. Without it, the cadence will sound as if it were a Imaj7 to IVMaj7 in the key of G. Try playing the cadences below with and without the pedal tone. The pedal note C provides the foundation for the listener to hear the F♯ (scale degree 7 of GMaj7) as a ♯11 (the characteristic pitch of Lydian mode).

Fig. 13.29. This Lydian cadence is more effective with a pedal tone.

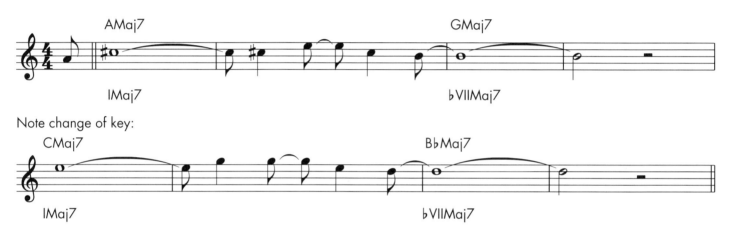

Fig. 13.30. "Lady Slipper" (R. Felts), original form

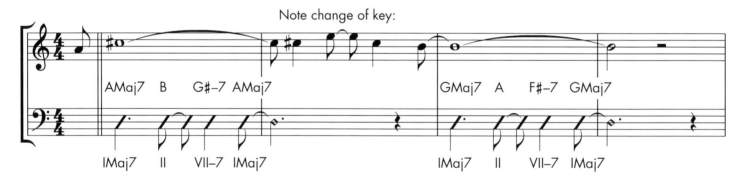

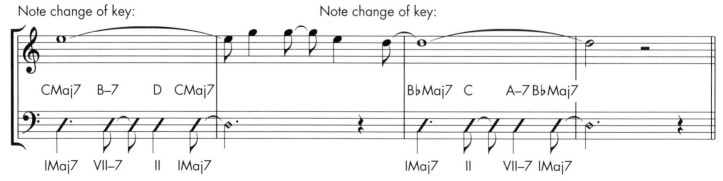

Fig. 13.31. "Lady Slipper," reharmonized with Lydian cadences

Fig. 13.32. "Nostalgia in Times Square" (C. Mingus), original form

The slower harmonic rhythm applied to the reharmonization below makes it easier to hear the modal cadences that support the melody. The use of tonic pedal tones in each key area also reinforces the modal color of each phrase.

Note the change of key. (Key changes often work well at the start of a new melodic phrase.) Using different modal key areas to support individual melodic phrases allows a modal texture to be maintained over a greater number of bars. Writing longer modal phrases makes it easier for the listener to appreciate the modal mood of your reharmonization.

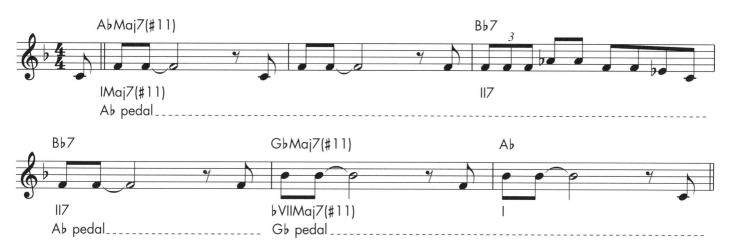

Fig. 13.33. "Nostalgia in Times Square," reharmonized with Lydian cadences

Later examples will also show a variety of modal cadences applied to different phrases in the same song: one phrase in D Dorian, followed by a second phrase in A Aeolian, followed by a third phrase in G Lydian, etc. (See modal reharmonization of "My Funny Valentine" later in this chapter.)

MIXOLYDIAN MODE: The I chord in Mixolydian mode is major (IMaj), dominant (I7), or dominant 7sus4 (I7sus4), and is the tonic chord of its key. The characteristic note of Mixolydian mode is ♭7 (B♭ in key of C).

Fig. 13.34. Mixolydian scale in C

Each of the cadential chords shown below contains the characteristic note. Moving to I with the following chord combinations will create cadences with a distinctive Mixolydian color.

As with all modes, notice whether the cadential chords are major or minor, and memorize the Roman numeral combinations shown in each modal key. You may use both triads and seventh chords, as indicated in the examples. For study purposes, consider each resolution to C as a separate cadence. Any or all of these combinations leading to the I, I7, or I7sus4 chord will produce a Mixolydian color.

Fig. 13.35. Mixolydian cadences

One- or two-chord cadences derived from the same modal scale may also be used to approach I or I7. Variations of triad and seventh chords may be used freely.

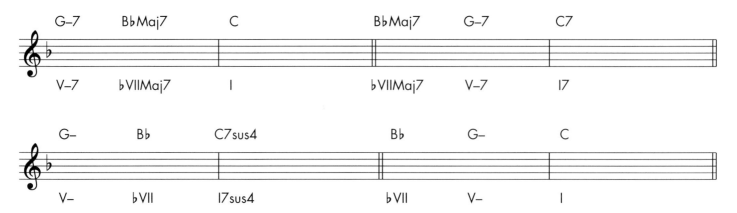

Fig. 13.36. Mixolydian cadence variations

In the reharmonization below, notice the change of harmonic rhythm in measure 4. The elongation of the I7 chord helps reinforce the modal color of the progression. Also notice the change of key in measure 5. Changing modal key areas to support individual phrases is often necessary to maintain a modal sound throughout a complete verse or chorus of a tune.

Fig. 13.37. "Nostalgia in Times Square," reharmonized with Mixolydian cadences

The example below is a good candidate for modal reharmonization because its melody is diatonic to a single scale. The original harmony includes a phrase in E Dorian followed by a modulation to the key of G major.

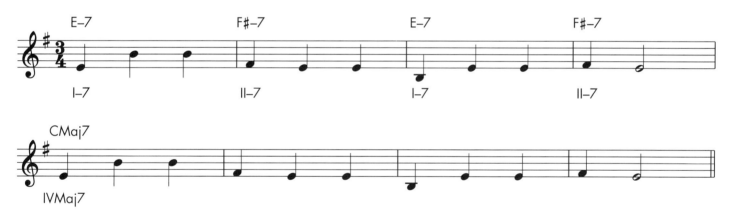

Fig. 13.38. "My Favorite Things" (R. Rodgers/O. Hammerstein), original form

Here, the two-measure harmonic rhythm on the I7 locks the Mixolydian color in place. The example uses Mixolydian cadence chords to approach I7.

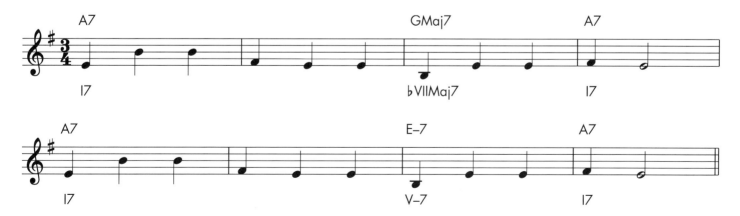

Fig. 13.39. "My Favorite Things," reharmonized with Mixolydian cadences

When working from a modal point of view, always emphasize the I by giving it a long duration or by using many repetitions of it. This will prevent the listener from hearing your modal phrase as part of related major key. Our ears are saturated with the sound of major-key chord patterns and will interpret chord patterns as part of a major key unless a modal key center is clearly established. Always place the I in strong rhythmic positions within the phrase, and consider supporting it with a tonic pedal tone.

Fig. 13.40. "My Funny Valentine" (R. Rodgers/L. Hart), original form

Below, the I chord is placed in strong rhythmic positions in the first phrase and is used repeatedly. The rhythmic emphasis and repetition of the I chord helps establish a clear tonal center. The elongation of the ♭VIIMaj7 cadence chord in the second phrase adds variety, while the support of the F pedal tone ensures that the phrase will be heard in the key of F.

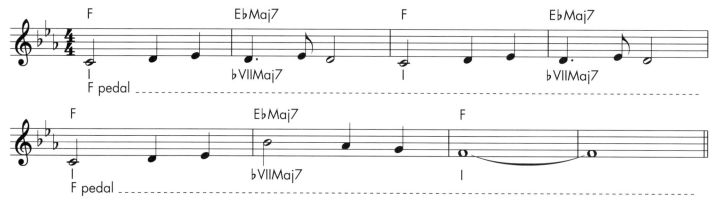

Fig. 13.41. "My Funny Valentine," reharmonized with Mixolydian cadences and a tonic pedal tone

The same phrase is harmonized below in the key of B♭ Mixolydian. Since the melody does not emphasize B♭ pitches, the B♭ pedal tone helps establish the B♭ tonality. The B♭ chords have long duration, are placed in the strong rhythmic positions, and are repeated often. All of these factors help us to hear the modal color.

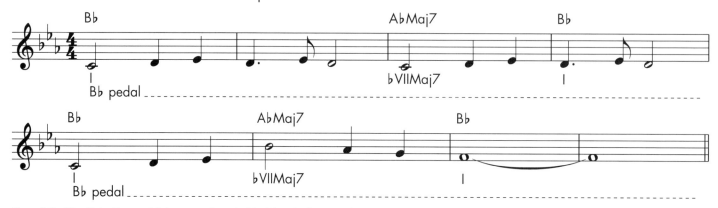

Fig. 13.42. "My Funny Valentine," with B♭ Mixolydian cadence

REHARMONIZING WITH SEVERAL MODES

You may choose to reharmonize an entire song modally. Songs with largely diatonic melodies are good candidates for this approach. However, it is rare to find a melody that can be successfully reharmonized with only a single mode and in a single key.

The examples that follow use several modes to reharmonize individual phrases. The modal key areas change as needed to harmonize melodic phrases.

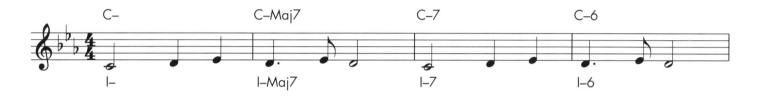

Fig. 13.43. "My Funny Valentine," original form

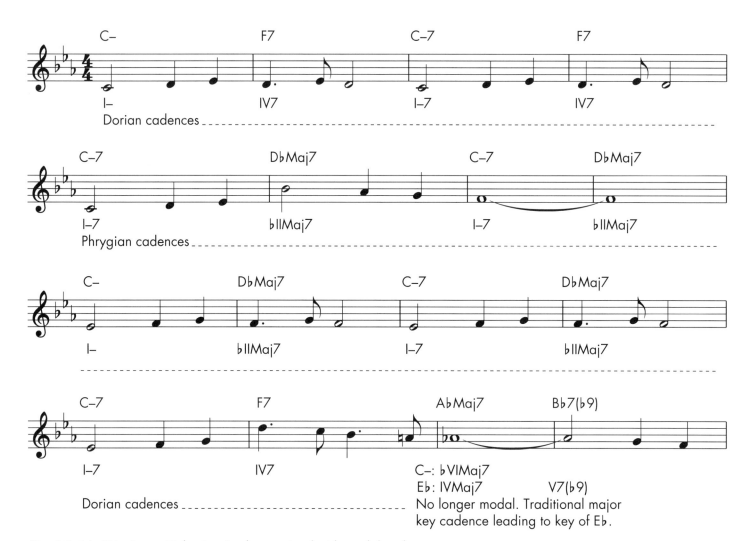

Fig. 13.44. "My Funny Valentine," reharmonized with modal cadences

Use your artistic discretion to determine which modes to use with a given melodic phrase and when to change keys and modes. Melody/harmony combinations will dictate which modes are technically possible for a specific phrase, but only your ears can determine which modal combinations work musically.

Sometimes, in the Lydian mode, you can write only a two-bar phrase before running into melody/harmony combinations that do not fit a Lydian tonality. Choosing to work the same phrase in Phrygian would allow for a full four-bar phrase before running into melody/harmony problems. In such a case, I would likely choose to work with the Phrygian mode, since longer modal phrases are easier for the listener to clearly recognize. Even in such a case, however, I might choose a key despite its short duration because of the "tastiness" of certain melody/harmony combinations and the location of these combinations within the overall phrase. Ultimately, it is the arranger's choice.

In the next example, the melody remains in the original key while the progression shifts to the key of F Dorian and A♭ Lydian. These modal cadences are possible because they do not clash with the melody.

Fig. 13.45. "My Funny Valentine," reharmonized with modal cadences

Note that key changes match melodic phrases. Below, the E♭ pedal tone in the third phrase reinforces the E♭ Mixolydian sound.

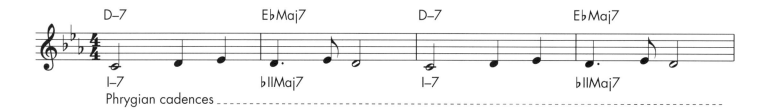

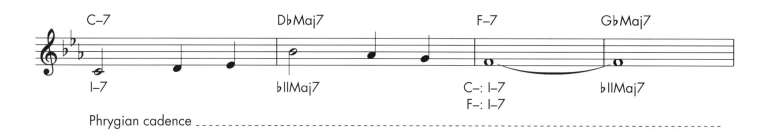

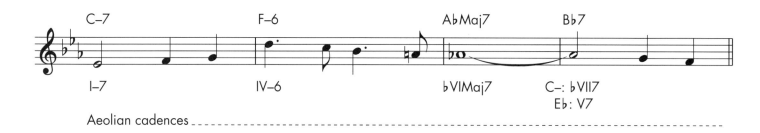

Fig. 13.46. "My Funny Valentine," reharmonized with modal cadences in various keys

EXERCISES

Using a variety of modal cadences, reharmonize the following examples. Identify the name of the mode and its key. Label each chord with Roman numerals.

Since all the melody notes of the example are diatonic to E♭ major, choose a new modal key based on this tonality. Try a variety: F Dorian, based on the second step of the original E♭ major key; G Phrygian, based on the third degree of E♭; A♭ Lydian, based on the fourth degree of E♭; B♭ Mixolydian, based on the fifth degree of E♭; or, C Aeolian, based on the sixth degree of E♭. These modes are appropriate because they share the same pitches as the melodic line.

EXERCISE 13.1

Original form:

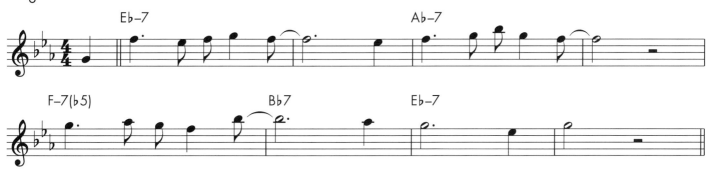

Your modal reharmonization 1:

Your modal reharmonization 2:

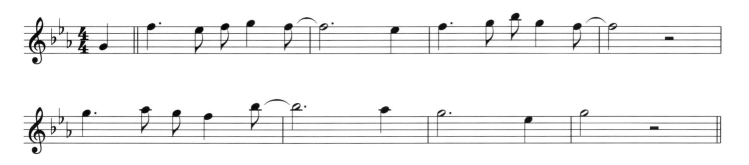

Using a variety of modal cadences, reharmonize the following examples. Identify the name of the mode and its key. Label each chord with Roman numerals.

Your modal reharmonization 3:

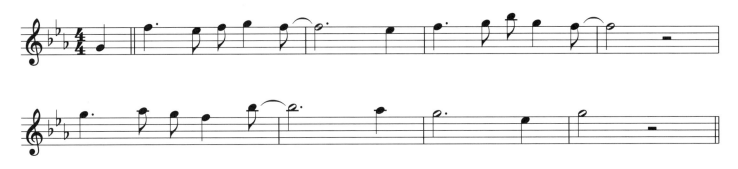

Your modal reharmonization 4:

Notice that B♮ is used two bars from the end of the phrase below. This note is chromatic to the key that is implied by the rest of the phrase. Since this is a very obvious chromatic pitch, it will cause unwanted melody/harmony combinations if you try to reharmonize it using a single key for the entire phrase. Therefore, change modal keys at this point. Pick a new mode that will include B and C♯ (D♭ enharmonic spelling). Since the phrase is short, emphasize the I of the new key with a tonic pedal tone. Study my example before creating your own.

EXERCISE 13.2

Original form:

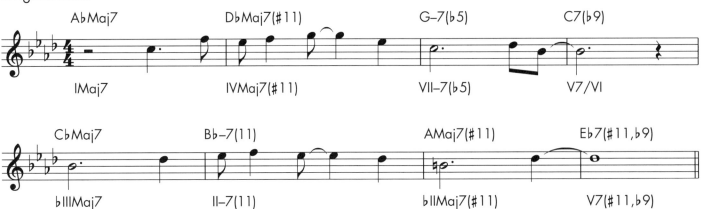

Sample reharmonization:

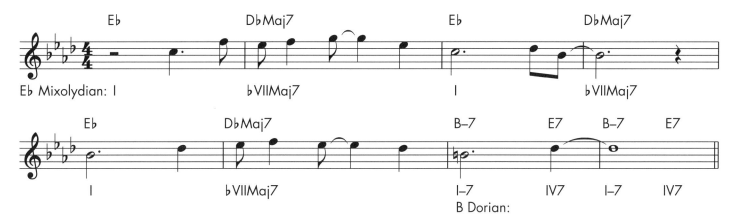

Your modal reharmonization 1:

Your modal reharmonization 2:

Your modal reharmonization 3:

Reharmonize the following example using modes related to C major (i.e., D Dorian, E Phrygian, F Lydian, G Mixolydian, or A Aeolian). Place the I chord of your chosen modal key in strong rhythmic positions and cadence to it using diatonic cadential chords. Refer to the cadential choices outlined earlier in this chapter. Identify the name of the mode and its key, and label each chord with Roman numerals.

EXERCISE 13.3

Original form:

Your modal reharmonization 1:

Your modal reharmonization 2:

Your modal reharmonization 3:

Your modal reharmonization 4:

HYBRID CHORD VOICINGS

Hybrid chords have two layers: a bass note and an upper chord layer that is separated from the bass note by at least a third. The bass note is not repeated anywhere in the upper layer. These chords are referred to by some players as "slash chords," since they are made up of a triad or a seventh chord, a slash symbol, and a bass note.

Fig. 14.1. Common examples of hybrid chords

These types of chord structures are also sometimes referred to as **hybrid voicings**, since they are closely related to traditional chord structures. They are deliberately structured to create an ambiguous sound. Ambiguous textures became popular in orchestral composition in the early part of the twentieth century and are related in a broad way to the artistic movement, impressionism.

Like impressionist artists that shun ultra-realistic visual representation, hybrid voicings, which by definition contain neither a major or minor third above the bass note, give an "impression" of a chord sound. The sound is open to personal interpretation by the listener. The special flavor of these voicings may be used to harmonize specific notes in a melody or to harmonize entire phrases.

Typically, in hybrid voicings, the upper chord layer is found:

    1. up a major second from the bass note

    2. down a major second from the bass note

    3. up a perfect fifth from the bass note

Less common hybrid voicings may also be found:

    4. up a tritone from the bass note

    5. up a minor second from the bass note

Examples of types 4 and 5 are shown in the next illustration.

Fig. 14.2. Other useful hybrid voicings

Hybrid structures of the type shown above produce an altered dominant sound. This altered dominant sound is produced when the notes in the chord voicing are derived from the altered dominant scale. The altered scale is described by different names in different texts, but contains the following pattern: 1, ♭9, ♯9, 3, ♯4 or ♭5, ♭6, ♭7, 1.

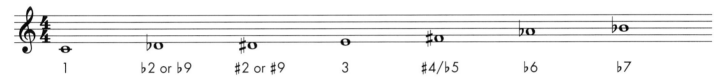

Fig. 14.3. Altered scale in C

The term "altered" is used because compared to a "normal" dominant scale (1, 9, 3, 4, 5, 6, ♭7), each of the notes except the crucial 1, 3, and ♭7 have been changed or altered.

To construct hybrid voicings of traditional chord structures:

1. Keep the root of the original chord.

2. Choose an **upper structure layer** that forms a major or minor triad or forms a major seventh, a minor seventh, or a dominant seventh. Avoid augmented, diminished, or minor 7(♭5) structures in the upper layer of hybrid chords since they tend to sound like more traditional chord voicings when combined with the bass note.

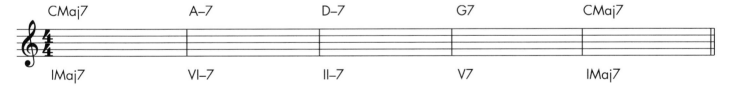

Fig. 14.4. Original form

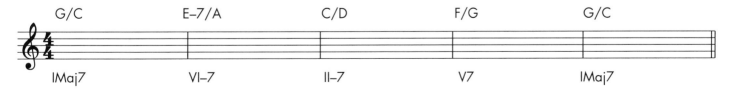

Fig. 14.5. Reharmonization using hybrid voicings of the original progression

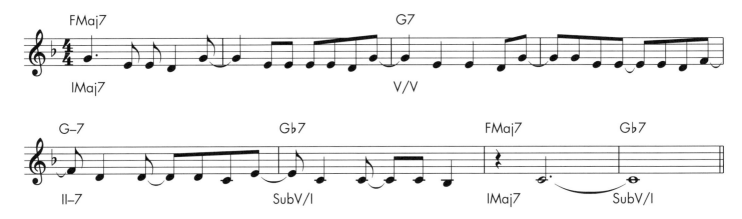

Fig. 14.6. "The Girl From Ipanema" (A.C. Jobim/V. De Moraes/N. Gimbel), original form

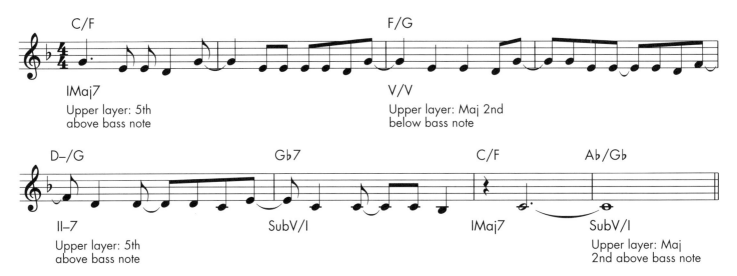

Fig. 14.7. "The Girl From Ipanema," reharmonized with hybrid chord voicings

Here is another example of reharmonization with hybrid chord voicings.

Fig. 14.8. "Bossa La Nuit" (R. Felts), original form

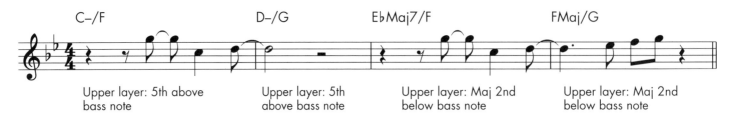

Fig. 14.9. "Bossa La Nuit," reharmonized with hybrid voicings

Hybrid voicings lose their effectiveness if melody notes form intervals of either a major or minor third above the bass note. Errors of several kinds are produced if a third is in the lead:

1. The melody note may produce an unwanted ♭9 interval with the upper layer of the hybrid chord.

2. The third above the bass note will destroy the ambiguous texture associated with this hybrid technique.

Fig. 14.10. "Lone Jack" (P. Metheny), original form

Below, the D♭ melody note (a minor third above the bass note) clashes with the upper layer of the hybrid voicing and disrupts the ambiguous texture associated with hybrid voicings.

Fig. 14.11. "Lone Jack," problematic reharmonization

A hybrid voicing often works well at the end of a phrase. The entire phrase need not be harmonized with hybrid chords.

Fig. 14.12. "Lydia's Fortune" (R. Felts), original form

Fig. 14.13. Hybrid chord voicing used at phrase ending provides contrast

Occasionally the same upper layer may be repeated over two different bass notes.

Fig. 14.14. "If You Knew" (R. Felts), original form

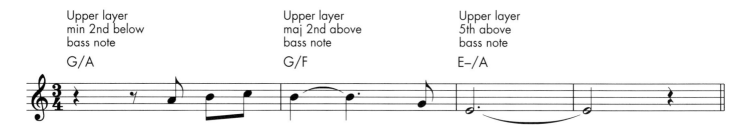

Fig. 14.15. "If You Knew," reharmonized with hybrid voicings

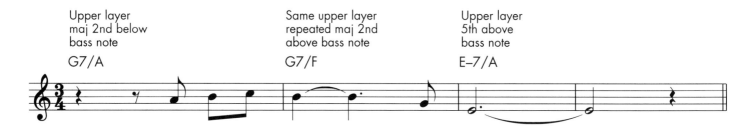

Fig. 14.16. The upper layer of a hybrid chord may be voiced as either a triad or a seventh chord.

Fig. 14.17. A given phrase may contain a mixture of both triads and seventh chords used in the upper layer of hybrid chord voicings.

EXERCISES

Use hybrid chord voicings to reharmonize the following examples.

EXERCISE 14.1

"Bossa La Nuit," original form

Your reharmonization 1:

Your reharmonization 2:

Your reharmonization 3:

EXERCISE 14.2

"Bossa La Nuit," original form

Your reharmonization 1:

Your reharmonization 2:

Your reharmonization 3:

Use hybrid chord voicings and other techniques of your choice to reharmonize the following examples.

EXERCISE 14.3

"New Year's Resolution" (R. Felts), original form

Your reharmonization 1:

Your reharmonization 2:

Your reharmonization 3:

EXERCISE 14.4

"New Year's Resolution," original form continued

Your reharmonization 1:

Your reharmonization 2:

Your reharmonization 3:

CONSTANT STRUCTURE PATTERNS

A **constant structure pattern** is a chord sequence in which all the chords share an identical quality but do not repeat the same root. Constant structure patterns may include sequences of major seventh chords, minor seventh chords, dominant seventh chords, or dominant 7sus4 chords.

Using a series of chords having the same quality but different roots focuses attention on the chord quality itself (texture) and on the root motion. Emphasizing texture and root motion at the expense of a clear-cut sense of key is a relatively recent development in music history. Using constant structures will therefore give a reharmonized phrase a certain impressionistic quality loosely related to twentieth-century film music and jazz.

Occasionally, constant structure patterns will have a clear analysis within a key (or a partial analysis within a key), but often they form phrases organized entirely on their textural sound.

CMaj7	EbMaj7	GbMaj7	EbMaj7	CMaj7
IMaj7	bIIIMaj7	Nonfunctional in the key	bIIIMaj7	IMaj7

Fig. 15.1. Constant structure phrase with partial analysis in the key of C major

CMaj7	EbMaj7	FMaj7	CMaj7
IMaj7	bIIIMaj7	IVMaj7	IMaj7

Fig. 15.2. Phrase with completely tonal analysis in the key of C major

G7sus4	A7sus4	Bb7sus4	G7sus4

Fig. 15.3. Constant structure phrase with consistent dominant 7sus4 quality with no clear tonal or key-related analysis

Constant structure chord progressions that lack key-related analyses often have a consistent pattern of motion in the bass. Below, the bass motion moves up and down in half steps.

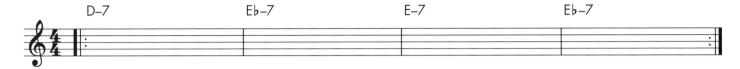

Fig. 15.4. Chords of consistent minor seventh quality with no clear tonal, key-related analysis

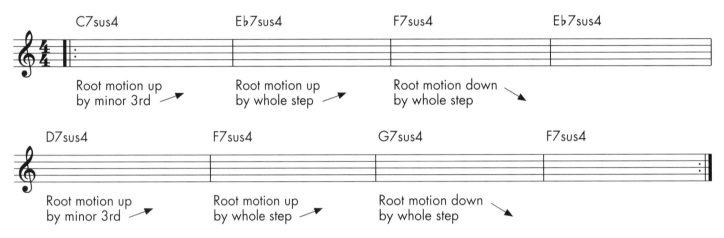

Fig. 15.5. Other structured patterns of bass motion

Use of structured patterns in the bass (consistent motion up or down by half steps, whole steps, or major or minor thirds) helps to organize the sound of constant structure progressions. Patterned, consistent root motion usually has a positive effect on the sound of constant structure progressions, but is not required. The consistent textural sound of constant structures and melody/harmony relationships form the primary organizational elements of this technique.

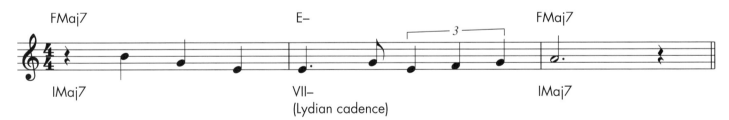

Fig. 15.6. "The Ten Worlds" (R. Felts), original form

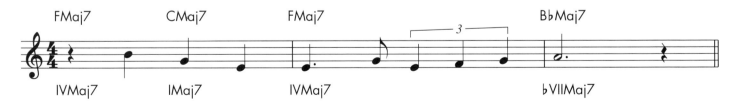

Fig. 15.7. "The Ten Worlds," reharmonized using constant structures

The constant structure dominant seventh sus4 chords in fig. 15.8 loosely outline I, IV, and V in the key of A, but are not clearly tonal.

Fig. 15.8. "The Ten Worlds," reharmonized using constant structures

The roots of the constant structure major seventh chords in the example below outline an F# diminished triad (F#, A, C). This progression is organized by the root motion but is not clearly tonal.

Fig. 15.9. "The Ten Worlds," reharmonized using constant structures

The roots of the constant structure chords in the example below outline a D triad: D, F#, A.

Fig. 15.10. Constant structure chords spell out D major triad

The roots of the constant structure chords in fig. 15.11 outline an Fmaj7 played in reverse order from the 13 (D) down to the root (F). These pitches, viewed as a chord, spell out FMaj7 (9, #11, 13). This overall structure gives coherence to the constant structure pattern. The lead in most of the chords is a tension; melodic tensions are a common part of this vocabulary.

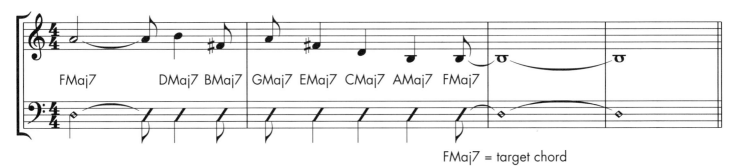

Fig. 15.11. Constant structure chords spell out FMaj7 chord with tensions

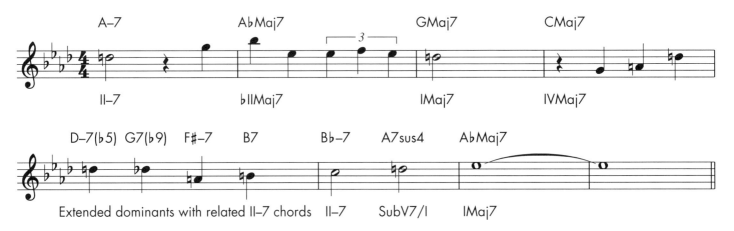

Fig. 15.12. "In Her Memory" (R. Felts), original form

The constant structure pattern in this reharmonization moves down stepwise from G to C, and then rises stepwise from C to A♭.

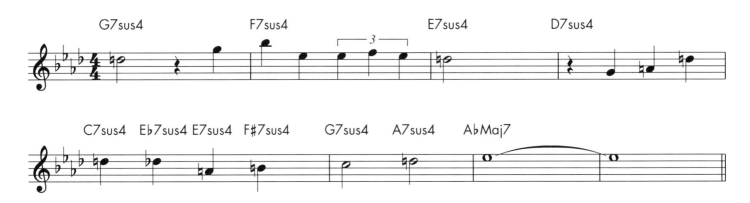

Fig. 15.13. "In Her Memory," reharmonized using constant structures

EXERCISES

Reharmonize the melodic examples below using constant structure progressions.

EXERCISE 15.1

"The Ten Worlds," original form

Your reharmonization 1:

Your reharmonization 2:

EXERCISE 15.2

"In Her Memory," original form

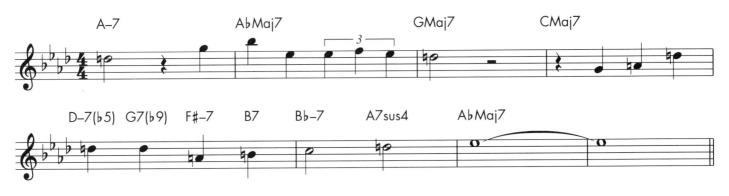

Your reharmonization 1:

Your reharmonization 2:

EXERCISE 15.3

"If You Knew," original form

Your reharmonization 1:

Your reharmonization 2:

Your reharmonization 3:

EXERCISE 15.4

"Habitual" (R. Felts), original form

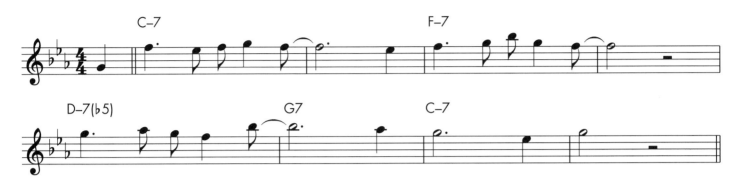

Your reharmonization 1:

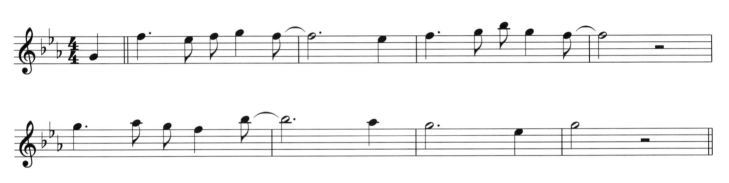

Your reharmonization 2:

COMBINING MODAL PATTERNS, HYBRID CHORD VOICINGS, AND CONSTANT STRUCTURES

Once you understand the basics, you may combine modal patterns, hybrid chord voicings, and constant structures.

Fig. 16.1. "The Ten Worlds," original form

Since its melody is completely diatonic, "The Ten Worlds" may be reharmonized by the various modes of the C major scale. I have chosen to reharmonize the original progression with a chord pattern taken from E Phrygian. The E–7 is placed in rhythmically strong measures 1 and 3 to create a tonal emphasis on E.

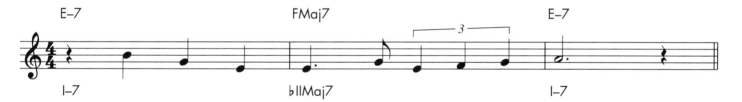

Fig. 16.2. Phrygian reharmonization

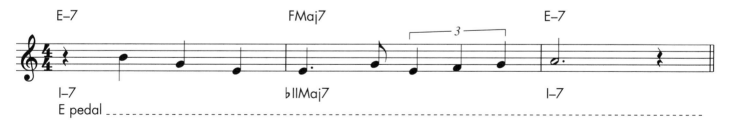

Fig. 16.3. Use of an E pedal tone strengthens the E Phrygian sound

Voicing all or some of the chords in the modal progression as hybrid structures develops the chord progression further. The G in the melody creates a mild dissonance with the F♯ in the B minor upper layer. You may choose to accept this relatively mild dissonance or avoid it by not using a hybrid voicing in the first measure.

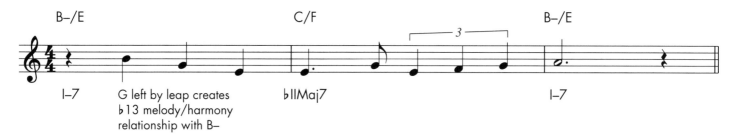

Fig. 16.4. Voicing chords as hybrids develops the chord progression.

The example below eliminates the clash between the G in the melody and the F♯ in the B minor upper layer by omitting a hybrid voicing in the first measure.

Fig. 16.5. Melody/harmony clash corrected in first measure

Hybrid voicings may also be supported by pedal tones.

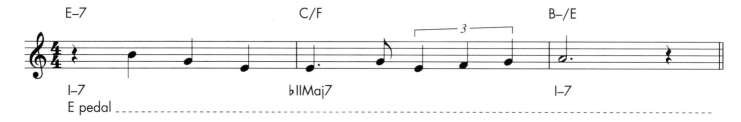

Fig. 16.6. Hybrid voicing with pedal tone

Sometimes all three approaches—modal patterns, hybrid voicings, and constant structures—can be applied to the same melodic fragment.

In fig. 16.7, the original example is reharmonized a second time with an A-G-A root motion. This root motion may be thought of as I-♭VII-I in the key of A minor (Aeolian).

Two other considerations were important in this choice:

    1. All melody notes within this fragment are diatonic to A minor.

    2. The melody ends on A in measure 3, which reinforces the modal character of the phrase.

Fig. 16.7. Reharmonization with an A Aeolian progression

Using hybrid voicings based on this modal phrase creates a variation.

Fig. 16.8. Hybrid voicings add variation to the modal phrase.

The examples below show further hybrid voicings that could be generated from the original A-7 to G chord pattern. (See chapter 14 to review hybrid construction.)

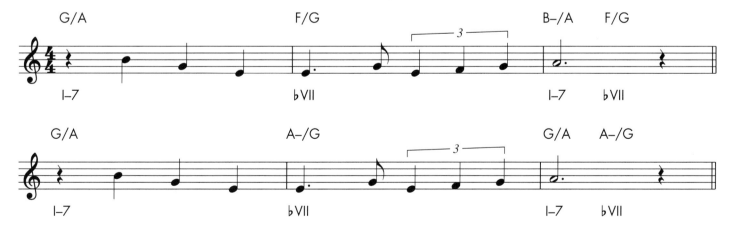

Fig. 16.9. Hybrid voicings: variations

Constant structure patterns may also be developed from a modal reharmonization. The phrases below show patterns developed from the original Aeolian modal idea (from the key of A Aeolian).

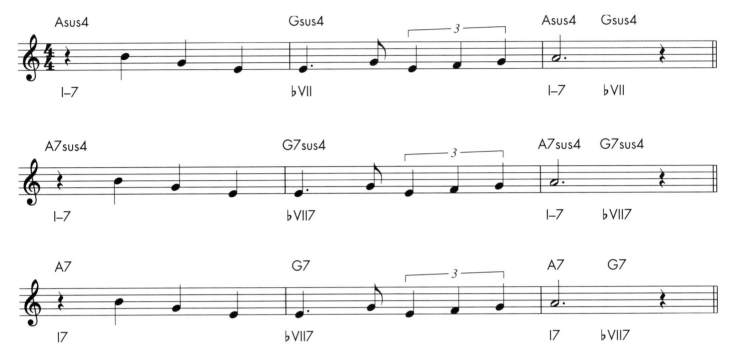

Fig. 16.10. Constant structure patterns developed from the root motion of an A Aeolian progression

Pedal tones or ostinato patterns can emphasize the implied tonality of constant structure examples. The use of an A pedal in the example below makes the phrase sound as if it is in the key of A, despite the ambiguous nature of the constant structure progression.

Fig. 16.11. Pedal tone emphasizes the A tonality

Using a G pedal tone creates a different color, while maintaining the same constant structures in the upper layer. Notice that the Gsus4 now sounds like a I chord when used with a G pedal tone.

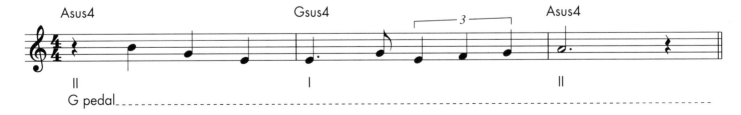

Fig. 16.12. G pedal tone adds color to constant structure pattern

If a melodic motive is repeated exactly or with minor variation, consider variations to the supporting chord progression.

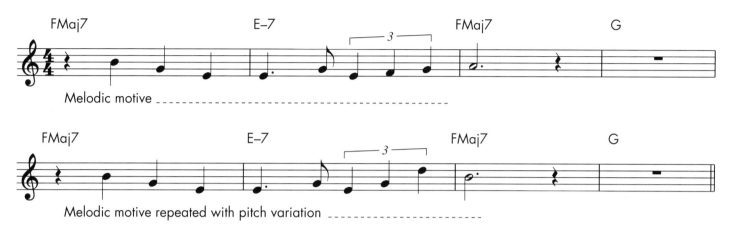

Fig. 16.13. "The Ten Worlds," original form

The example below uses minor seventh chords as constant structures with an A pedal in measures 1–4 and dominant 7sus4 chords as constant structures with a G pedal in measures 5–8. This introduces some variety, yet maintains a similar chordal texture throughout the phrase.

Fig. 16.14. Constant structure pattern using A to G root motion, inspired by A Aeolian

Fig. 16.15. Constant structure pattern using A to G root motion, inspired by G Dorian

To summarize, modal harmony, hybrid voicings, and constant structures may be used interchangeably. To use this approach, choose a melody that is largely diatonic. Then, reharmonize the melody using modal chord patterns.

Options:
- Revoice the chords of the modal progression as hybrids.
- Use the root motion from the modal progression as the root motion of a constant structure pattern.
- Use pedal tones or ostinato patterns to support any progression produced by these means.

Here's how it works:

1. Choose a song fragment that contains a diatonic melody. The fragment below could be diatonic to more than one key. Any key that contains an E♭ but not a G♭ would work. This fragment could be considered part of B♭ major, E♭ major, or A♭ major key signatures. Modal chord patterns diatonic to these key signatures could then be used as reharmonizations of the phrase.

Fig. 16.16. "Bossa La Nuit," original form

2. Reharmonize the original chord pattern with a new modal progression. Here, D Phrygian, which is diatonic to the key signature of B♭, works smoothly with the melody.

Fig. 16.17. "Bossa La Nuit," with D Phrygian

Optional: Revoice the modal progression using hybrid chords.

Fig. 16.18. "Bossa La Nuit," revoiced with hybrid chords

Optional: Reharmonize the modal progression using constant structures that use the same root motion.

Fig. 16.19. "Bossa La Nuit," with constant structures

Optional: Support the reharmonized progression with a pedal tone.

Fig. 16.20. "Bossa La Nuit," with pedal tones

EXERCISES

Reharmonize the following examples using combinations of modal chord patterns, hybrid voicings, and constant structures. Choose freely among the techniques to produce a reharmonized version you like. (I often select chords that produce tensions in the melodic lead of constant structure patterns. I also aim for constant structure patterns that have a clear intervallic organization of the root motion.) Try to maintain a specific technique for several bars at a time.

Modal phrases and constant structure examples normally require repetition to develop a clear meaning in the listener's ear. If you seek a strong modal quality, repeat the I chord and its characteristic cadential chords often to drive the point home. Use of a tonic pedal tone or tonic ostinato will help to reinforce the sense of modal tonality.

Hybrid chords may occasionally be used as isolated structures within phrases, but they acquire a stronger textural personality when used in a series. A series of hybrid chords produces a stronger impressionistic effect than an isolated hybrid voicing.

EXERCISE 16.1

"Bossa La Nuit," original form

Your reharmonization 1:

Your reharmonization 2:

Your reharmonization 3:

EXERCISE 16.2

"The Ten Worlds," original form

Your reharmonization 1:

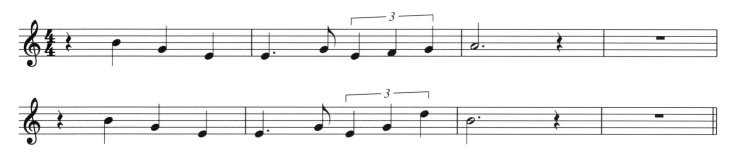

Your reharmonization 2:

Your reharmonization 3:

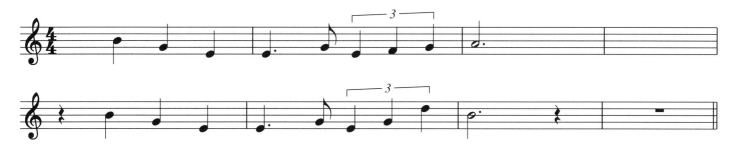

Your reharmonization 4:

REFERENCE EXAMPLES

The following examples show ways the exercises in chapters 1–16 *might* be completed. While there are no "right" answers in reharmonization, looking at these will help you determine whether you're on the right track with your own reharmonizations.

CHAPTER 3

EXERCISE 3.1, p. 35
Reharmonization 1:

Extended dominant 7ths with related II-7 chords leading to an A-7 target

Reharmonization 2:

Extended dominants with related II-7 chords
Root motion of some II-V combinations is chromatic.
A7 leads to D7 by skipping over A-7

EXERCISE 3.2, p. 35
Reharmonization 1:

Reharmonization 2:

Eb7 leads to D7 by skipping over A-7

EXERCISE 3.3, p. 36
Reharmonization 1:

Reharmonization 2:

EXERCISE 3.4, p. 36
Reharmonization 1:

Reharmonization 2:

CHAPTER 4

EXERCISE 4.1, p. 42
Reharmonization 1:

EXERCISE 4.2, p. 43
Reharmonization 1:

Reharmonization 2:

EXERCISE 4.3, p. 43
Roman numeral analysis:

EXERCISE 4.4, p. 44
Reharmonization 1:

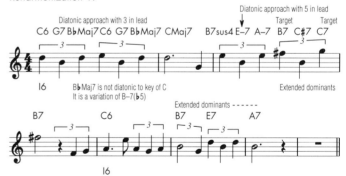

Reharmonization 2:

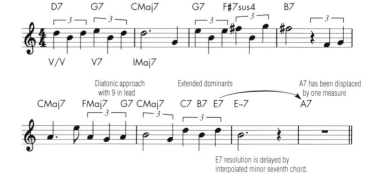

Chapter 5

EXERCISE 5.1, p. 50

Reharmonization 1:

Reharmonization 2:

Reharmonization 3:

EXERCISE 5.2, p. 51

Reharmonization 1:

Reharmonization 2:

Reharmonization 3:

EXERCISE 5.3, p. 52

Reharmonization 1:

Reharmonization 2:

Reharmonization 3:

CHAPTER 6

EXERCISE 6.1, p. 62

Reharmonization 1:

Reharmonization 2:

Reharmonization 3:

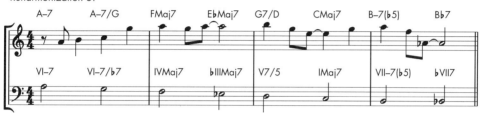

EXERCISE 6.2, p. 63

Reharmonization 1:

Reharmonization 2:

Reharmonization 3:

Reharmonization 1:

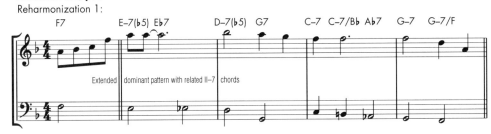

Reharmonization 2:

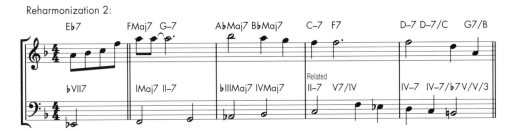

Reharmonization 3:

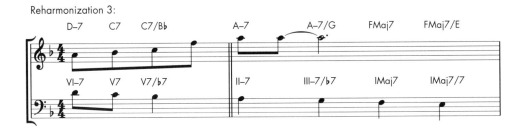

CHAPTER 7
EXERCISE 7.1, p. 71

EXERCISE 7.2, p. 72

EXERCISE 7.3, p. 72
"There! I've Said It Again" (D. Mann/R. Evans)

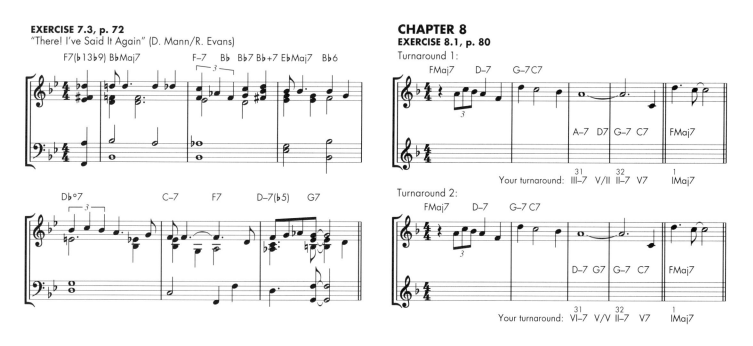

CHAPTER 8
EXERCISE 8.1, p. 80

EXERCISE 8.2, p. 80

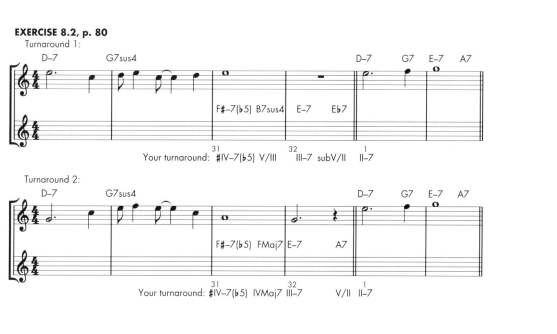

EXERCISE 8.3, p. 81

EXERCISE 8.4, p. 84

EXERCISE 9.3, p. 92
Extended ending 1:

III–7   V7/II   II–7   subV/I   IMaj7

Extended ending 2:

bIIIMaj7   bVIMaj7   bIIMaj7   I6

EXERCISE 9.4, p. 93
Extended ending 1:

bVIMaj7   bVIIMaj7   subV/I   I–7

Extended ending 2:
Constant structure major 7th chords moving with strong root motion:

bIIMaj7   G:bIIMaj7   IMaj7

EXERCISE 9.5, p. 94
Note that in bar 31 of the extended ending, the first chord is a standard deceptive chord, a variation of VI–7.
Also notice the use of strong root motion throughout the interlude.

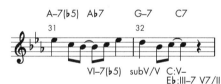

VI–7(b5)   subV/V   C:V–
Eb:III–7   V7/II

Beginning of same
tune in a new key:

II–7   subV/I   Eb:IMaj7   II–7   V7   I–

EXERCISE 9.6, p. 94
In bar 31, the first chord is a standard deceptive chord, a variation of III–7.
Also notice the use of strong root motion throughout the interlude.

bIIIMaj7   bIIMaj7

Beginning of same
tune in a new key:

II–7   V7   III–7   V7/II   II–7   V7
B:subV/I   IMaj7

CHAPTER 10
EXERCISE 10.1, p. 102

EXERCISE 10.2, p. 102

179

EXERCISE 10.3, p. 103

EXERCISE 10.4, p. 103

EXERCISE 10.5, p. 104

EXERCISE 10.6, p. 104

CHAPTER 11
EXERCISE 11.1, p. 111

"An August Moon" (R. Felts)
Reharmonization 1:

Reharmonization 2:

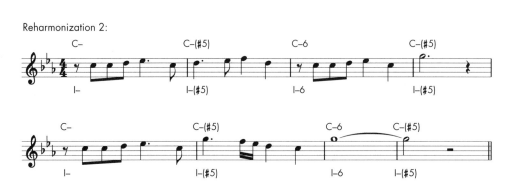

EXERCISE 11.2, p. 112

"Homecoming" (R. Felts)
Reharmonization 1:

Reharmonization 2:

CHAPTER 12

EXERCISE 12.1, p. 120

EXERCISE 12.2, p. 120

EXERCISE 12.3, p. 121

EXERCISE 12.4, p. 121

EXERCISE 12.5, p. 121

EXERCISE 12.6, p. 122

EXERCISE 12.7, p. 122

CHAPTER 13

EXERCISE 13.1, p. 141-142

EXERCISE 13.2, p. 142-143

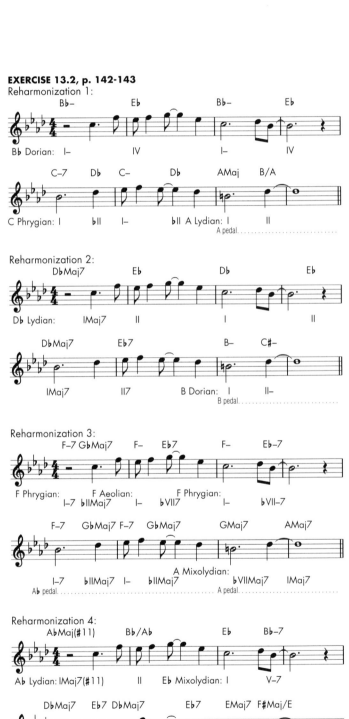

EXERCISE 14.4, p. 154
"New Year's Resolution"
Reharmonization 1:

Hybrid
of G–7

Hybrid of F–7, a
substitute for A♭Maj7

Hybrid voicings of the original chord changes

Reharmonization 2:

Hybrid of G7
I7

Hybrid of D–7
V–7
Mixolydian pattern

Hybrid
of B♭7

Hybrid
of B7

Hybrid
of C7(alt)

Hybrid
of D♭7

Above pattern derived from ascending bass line.

Reharmonization 3:

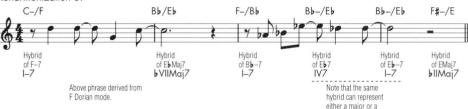

Hybrid
of F–7
I–7

Hybrid
of E♭Maj7
♭VIIMaj7

Hybrid
of B♭–7
I–7

Hybrid
of E♭7
IV7

Hybrid
of E♭–7
I–7

Hybrid
of EMaj7
♭IIMaj7

Above phrase derived from
F Dorian mode.

Note that the same
hybrid can represent
either a major or a
minor chord.

CHAPTER 15

EXERCISE 15.1, p. 159
"The Ten Worlds"
Reharmonization 1:

D7sus4   E7sus4   D7sus4

I   II   I

Root motion derived
from Dorian mode

Reharmonization 2:

A7sus4 G7sus4 D7sus4 A7sus4 G7sus4   A7sus4

I   ♭VII   IV   I   ♭VII   I

Root motion pattern loosely
related to key of A Dorian

EXERCISE 15.2, p. 160
"In Her Memory"
Reharmonization 1:

(Bars 1-3 inspired by D Phrygian; Bars 4-8 inspired by A Dorian)

D–7   E♭–7   D–7   A–7

D Phrygian: I   ♭II   I   A Dorian: I

B–7   A–7   B–7   C–7

II   I   II   ♭III

Reharmonization 2:
Constant structures based on chord tones of F–7(9), used in reverse order:

GMaj7   E♭Maj7   CMaj7   A♭Maj7 FMaj7

GMaj7   E♭Maj7 CMaj7 A♭Maj7

EXERCISE 15.3, p. 161
"If You Knew"
Reharmonization 1:

Use of 9ths in lead of the last two chords lends unity to the phrase.

B7sus4   A7sus4   D7sus4

Reharmonization 2:
Constant structures using strong root motion: whole steps and 4th/5th

D7sus4   E7sus4   A7sus4   B7sus4

Reharmonization 3:
Constant structure minor 7th chords moving down by stepwise root motion;
inspired by bass line reharmonization technique.

F#–7   E–7   D–7   C#–7

EXERCISE 15.4, p. 162
"Habitual" (R. Felts)
Reharmonization 1:
Constant structure pattern inspired by root motion found in Dorian mode:

F7sus4   G7sus4

I   II

F7sus4   E♭7sus4   F7sus4

I   ♭VII   I

Reharmonization 2:
Constant structure chords chosen to create mostly T9 or T11 in melody of each chord:

B♭7sus4   E♭7sus4

F7sus4   D7sus4 B♭7sus4 D7sus4

CHAPTER 16
EXERCISE 16.1, p. 170
"Bossa La Nuit"
Reharmonization 1:

Hybrid voicings derived from the original chord changes:

Reharmonization 2:

Chord pattern derived from C Dorian scale:

Reharmonization 3:

Pattern of root motion derived from F Mixolydian scale. Hybrid voicings then constructed on F Mixolydian roots.
In simple form, these voicings are: F7 to EbMaj7.

EXERCISE 16.2, p. 171
"The Ten Worlds"
Reharmonization 1:

C Lydian progression. C pedal tone can be used to strengthen the key sound of this example.

Reharmonization 2:

Step 1: Support melody with E Phrygian progression.

Step 2: Rewrite "normal" chords as hybrid voicings.

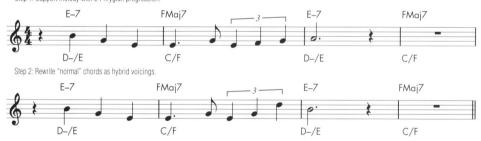

Reharmonization 3:

Constant structure pattern derived from F#°7 chord.

Reharmonization 4:

Constant structure progression used in Reharmonization 3 revoiced with hybrid voicings.
Roots are the same in both examples.

Glossary

Approach chord	A chord that provides a sense of harmonic movement to a target chord.
Cadence	A combination of one or two chords that provides a sense of harmonic resolution to a target chord.
Diatonic chords	Chord structures made up of notes derived from a single scale or mode.
Duration	The number of beats allocated to a chord.
Extended dominants	A series of dominant chords whose roots move down by intervals of a perfect fifth, minor second, or some combination of these intervals.
Harmonic rhythm	The number of beats allocated to a chord. One or two beats per chord is considered fast harmonic rhythm, while four, eight, or more beats per chord is slow harmonic rhythm.
Hybrid chords	Chord structures that contain three or four notes above a bass note. Measuring up from the bass note, no intervals of a third are found, and the bass note itself is not repeated in the upper structure layer.
Interpolated or interrupting chord	A chord of short duration, placed between a dominant approach chord and a target chord. The interpolated chord usually has a minor seventh or V7sus4 quality.
Lead	Melody notes, as found in a lead sheet, or the top note in a chord voicing.
Pedal	A sustained pitch used to support and accompany melodic lines and chord progressions. The sustained pitch is most often placed in the bass register and functions as I or V of its key.
Target chord	A chord chosen by a writer as an important structural element in the musical phrase. Any chord may be chosen as a target, but target chords are often the last or next-to-last chord of a phrase.
Tritone	The interval distance of three whole steps. Also known as an augmented fourth or diminished fifth. This interval combination tends to sound restless or unstable, and it provides a sense of motion when found in musical phrases and chord structures.
Upper structure layer	The top three or four notes of a nontraditional chord voicing. (See "Hybrid chords.")
Voice leading	The process of smoothly connecting notes from chord to chord with a blended, textural sound.

INDEX OF CREDITS

OOLS FOR DJs

**TURNTABLE TECHNIQUE:
THE ART OF THE DJ**
▶ by Stephen Webber
0449482 Book/2-Record Set $34.95

TURNTABLE BASICS ▶ by Stephen Webber
0449514 Book $9.95

VITAL VINYL, VOLUMES 1-5
▶ by Stephen Webber
12" records
0449491 Volume 1: Needle Juice $15.95
0449492 Volume 2: Turntablist's Toolkit.......$15.95
0449493 Volume 3: Rockin' the House $15.95
0449494 Volume 4: Beat Bomb $15.95
0449495 Volume 5: Tech Tools for DJs $15.95

TOOLS FOR DJs SUPERPACK
▶ by Stephen Webber
0449529 Includes Turntable Technique book/2-record
set and all 5 Vital Vinyl records (a $115 value!) ..$99.95

ERKLEE PRACTICE METHOD

Get Your Band Together

BASS ▶ by Rich Appleman and John Repucci
0449427 Book/CD...$14.95

DRUM SET ▶ by Ron Savage and
asey Scheuerell
0449429 Book/CD...$14.95

GUITAR ▶ by Larry Baione
0449426 Book/CD...$14.95

KEYBOARD ▶ by Russell Hoffmann and
aul Schmeling
0449428 Book/CD...$14.95

ALTO SAX ▶ by Jim Odgren and Bill Pierce
0449437 Book/CD...$14.95

TENOR SAX ▶ by Jim Odgren and Bill Pierce
0449431 Book/CD...$14.95

TROMBONE ▶ by Jeff Galindo
0449433 Book/CD...$14.95

TRUMPET ▶ by Tiger Okoshi and Charles
ewis
0449432 Book/CD...$14.95

ERKLEE INSTANT SERIES

BASS ▶ by Danny Morris
449502 Book/CD..$14.95

DRUM SET ▶ by Ron Savage
449513 Book/CD..$14.95

GUITAR ▶ by Tomo Fujita
449522 Book/CD..$14.95

KEYBOARD ▶ by Paul Schmeling and
ave Limina
449525 Book/CD..$14.95

IMPROVISATION SERIES

BLUES IMPROVISATION COMPLETE ▶
by Jeff Harrington ▶ Book/CD Packs
50449486 Bb Instruments $19.95
50449488 C Bass Instruments $19.95
50449425 C Treble Instruments $19.95
50449487 Eb Instruments $19.95

A GUIDE TO JAZZ IMPROVISATION
▶ by John LaPorta ▶ Book/CD Packs
50449439 C Instruments $16.95
50449441 Bb Instruments $16.95
50449442 Eb Instruments $16.95
50449443 Bass Clef $16.95

MUSIC TECHNOLOGY

ARRANGING IN THE DIGITAL WORLD
▶ by Corey Allen
50449415 Book/GM disk $19.95

**FINALE: AN EASY GUIDE TO MUSIC
NOTATION** ▶ by Thomas E. Rudolph and
Vincent A. Leonard, Jr.
50449501 Book/CD-ROM $59.95

**PRODUCING IN THE HOME STUDIO
WITH PRO TOOLS** ▶ by David Franz
50449526 Book/CD-ROM $34.95

RECORDING IN THE DIGITAL WORLD
▶ by Thomas E. Rudolph and
Vincent A. Leonard, Jr.
50449472 Book $29.95

MUSIC BUSINESS

**HOW TO GET A JOB IN THE MUSIC &
RECORDING INDUSTRY**
▶ by Keith Hatschek
50449505 Book $24.95

THE SELF-PROMOTING MUSICAN
▶ by Peter Spellman
50449423 Book $24.95

THE MUSICIAN'S INTERNET
▶ by Peter Spellman
50449527 Book $24.95

REFERENCE

COMPLETE GUIDE TO FILM SCORING
▶ by Richard Davis
50449417 Book $24.95

THE CONTEMPORARY SINGER
▶ by Anne Peckham
50449438 Book/CD...$24.95

ESSENTIAL EAR TRAINING
▶ by Steve Prosser
50449421 Book $14.95

MODERN JAZZ VOICINGS ▶ by Ted
Pease and Ken Pullig
50449485 Book/CD...$24.95

**THE NEW MUSIC THERAPIST'S
HANDBOOK, SECOND EDITION**
▶ by Suzanne B. Hanser
50449424 Book $29.95

POP CULTURE

INSIDE THE HITS
▶ by Wayne Wadhams
50449476 Book $29.95

**MASTERS OF MUSIC:
CONVERSATIONS WITH
BERKLEE GREATS** ▶ by Mark Small and
Andrew Taylor
50449422 Book $24.95

SONGWRITING

MELODY IN SONGWRITING
▶ by Jack Perricone
50449419 Book $19.95

MUSIC NOTATION ▶ by Mark McGrain
50449399 Book $19.95

**SONGWRITING: ESSENTIAL GUIDE
TO LYRIC FORM AND STRUCTURE**
▶ by Pat Pattison
50481582 Book $14.95

**SONGWRITING: ESSENTIAL GUIDE
TO RHYMING** ▶ by Pat Pattison
50481583 Book $14.95